Living BIG: Bold, Inspired, & Gifted

Shattering the Looking Glass to Releaase the Greatness Within

Verna Mayers-Fakunle

Copyright © 2021 Verna Mayers-Fakunle

Unless otherwise noted, all Scriptures are taken from the Holy Bible, New King James Version, copyright 2009, Thomas Nelson Inc. Publishers.

ISBN: 978-0-578-89988-6

Library of Congress Control Number:2021908081
Printed in the United States of America

Contact Me:
www.vernamayersfakunle.com
info@vernamayersfakunle.com

To my amazing Heavenly Father, the one who loves, guides, and sustains me. Thank you for creating me and equipping me to do the work you've purposed and designed me to do.

And to the memory of those who have left a legacy upon which my faith, values, tenacity, and wisdom have been built: my earthly father, Lealather Mayers, II; my grandparents, Lealather Mayers II and Annie Mae Mayers and Leon C. and Juanita Philippine Robinson Ferguson; and my wonderfully amazing aunts who gifted this world with a true spirit of servanthood, Dorothy Augustus and Margaret Mayers.

Acknowledgments

This book is the result of a long journey with much time spent in prayer and communion with my Heavenly Father, as well as with the guidance, love, and prayers of some people I am blessed to love and know.

To my loving and supportive husband, Olawale Fakunle. Thank you for showing me what true love is and for always being my rock and strength. You continue to show me through your actions every day how much you cherish me. I thank God for you and the gifts you bring to our marriage and to the world. I wake up each day feeling so very blessed to "do life" with you every day.

To my amazing mom, Christine Mayers, mere words cannot describe how blessed I am to have you as my mother. I am in awe of your complete and absolute love for me and for our entire family. Your example of grace, dignity, and strength will forever serve as a true legacy of what a godly woman exemplifies. I can only hope to leave as impactful a mark on the world as your sweet spirit, kind heart, and caring attitude are doing every day.

To the two gems of my heart, LeShay and Domevlo, you bring me so much joy. I am so blessed to have been gifted with the chance to grow "with" you and raise you as your bonus parent. Through our ups and downs, tests and trials, upsets and come backs, we have always been each other's greatest fans. I will forever and eternally be there to love you with my entire heart and soul. I pray you will forever be inspired by the life I live before you and remember to always stay grounded in the love God has for you. I am proud of your continued journeys and know there is so much greater God has for each of you.

To my brothers Lealather Mayers, III and Chris Mayers and to my sister, Michelle Mayers, thank you for your love and support. No matter what, I know I can always depend on you three for laughter, support, reminding me to "keep it real", and for being the original members of my power posse.

To my amazing Sistefriend, Tonya Nash, your encouragement and willingness to listen to me, talk me down from the ledge while at the same time pushing me to keep forging forward, and guide me through this process means so much to me. Thank you for your brutally honest insight into my writing and for challenging me to give more than I ever thought I could. I appreciate you, love you, and thank God for divinely connecting me to you.

Last but certainly not least, thank you to to everyone who has been gracious enough to invest in my story . Those who will reach beyond their own misperceptions of themselves and the ones cast upon them by others to see themselves through the eyes of our Creator. You have inspired me to keep dreaming, pushing forward, and walking in purpose. Let's LIVE **BIG** from this day foreward!

Contents

Introduction

For most of my life, I have dreamed big dreams: one after another, after another, after another. However, throughout my time here on earth, I have allowed every single one of those big dreams to expire into the abyss of unrealized potential and opportunity. To most people, I seem to be the kind of person who goes after what she wants, no holds barred. However, not many people, I dare venture to say, no one at all, would ever be able to guess how many life-long goals and dreams I have never been dedicated, committed, or ambitious enough to pursue.

Let's see, there's becoming a pediatrician, opening my own restaurant, building my own hotel, learning how to fly an airplane, being independently wealthy, developing a program to help young plus size girls build self-esteem and help them live loud and proud. Those are just a few but trust me there are quite a bit more. What does your list include? If you're being honest, I am sure you can also name quite a few just like me. Please don't feel bad however because we all have them!

As I got older, my list just seemed to get BIGGER every year and many of those dreams became a shallow memory in the distant past. I simply gave up on them when they became in my mind another unreachable goal that was too hard and required to much effort on my part. Always there was some obstacle I couldn't get around, some bridge I couldn't cross, and some mountain I couldn't climb. So, I simply gave up on them. Sound familiar?

I'm pretty sure most of you picked up this book looking for some new revelation on how to get moving and begin to build the life you've dreamed of. Well guess what? So was I! I read books, I watched self-help, motivational and inspirational videos, I went to lectures, I sought counsel of peers and professionals who seemed to be successful at having all the things they wanted in life. And here is what I learned...everything you need to fulfill every one of your BIG dreams...already lives within you! Sounds simple, doesn't it? How I wish it truly was, but it isn't.

On this journey called my life, I have come to realize that nothing that seems simple is ever as easy as it seems. Positioning yourself to move from a dreamer to an achiever takes hard work. Realizing the truth of this statement and understanding how to apply it to my own life is a path I am still walking every day. There is no quick fix, there is no set scheduled moment in time when you finally "get it" and your world miraculously transforms into perfection. Living in the fullness of your true power, must become something you breathe, live, embody, and thirst for everyday of your life.

There are some fundamental truths that I would like to explore with you in this journey to unleashing the beast of potential that rests inside you. This I believe is my God-ordained purpose for writing this book. It is my sincere prayer that sharing my testimony and my process to healing and living my own BIG (Bold,

> "
> Living in the fullness of your true power, must become something you breathe, live, embody, and thirst for everyday of your life.
> "

Inspired, & Gifted) life will help others change their lives and the lives of those around them.

So as an avid reader and book afficionado, if I was you and I was reading this book right now, the question I would be asking is, what makes this book different from the million other self-help books that are on the market right now? I mean you're no T.D. Jakes, Joel Osteen, Joyce Myers, Oprah Winfrey, or Michelle Obama. You're not an entertainer or a celebrity, as a matter of fact, do I even know you? And my response would be a resounding YES, you definitely know me! I'm right where you are, I'm learning, growing, maturing, and transforming right along with you as I write this book. That's what makes me different. I haven't arrived! Heck, there are days when I don't even start the car.

I am not professing to be an expert. This book is without a doubt being written to help people who like me have been afraid to walk boldly in the essence of who they were designed to be and before it can ever minster to you it HAS to minister to ME. I am walking this path of self-realization right along with you and openly sharing my journey with you through the process in hopes that you will gain valuable insight to change your life for the better. I am putting every part of me on display unashamedly in order that through my own journey you will be able to find strength, encouragement, and renewed commitment to YOU! My earnest prayer is that by the time you have completed this book, you will feel powerful, passionate, and poised to achieve those BIG (Bold, Inspired, & Gifted) dreams you have given up on and even those you have yet to imagine. Seven tenents I pray you understand and devote to implementing in your everyday lives are:

1. Facing YOUR Truth: The View Through the Looking Glass
2. Being the best YOU, you can be, not the YOU others expect you to be.
3. Embracing the positives and changing the negatives.
4. Releasing the Past, Walking into YOUR future!
5. Celebrating YOU! Small Steps Really Matter.
6. Pursuing YOUR passion, Finding YOUR purpose.
7. Saddle Up YOUR Power Posse.

Each chapter ends with a prayer, big step exercise, and journal entry. Feel free to repeat them and use them as often as you need until you have unleashed all that you have held within.

Chapter One

BIG Vision: Do You See What I See?
FACING YOUR TRUTH: THE LOOKING GLASS

We all have spent time looking in mirrors throughout the course of our lives. Most of the time, we don't think about it. I mean mirrors serve a purpose and looking in them usually is just a routine we do every day. Mirrors function to help us see things that we are not able to see in the physical. They bring us face to face with the reality of who we really are. WHO I see when I look in the mirror represents the physical part of me; WHAT I see is labeled the inner workings of all that is Verna, the spiritual, the mental, and the emotional.

Can you imagine getting ready to leave the house and risking not checking to be sure you present yourself to the world in the way you want? I know I can't! The mirror has been my saving grace on more occasions than I care to admit, I mean without it, the risk of showing up somewhere looking crazy is a major fear. Granted looking my best can be subjective and my definition could differ from someone else's but checking the mirror to be sure my hair is done, my face is clear, and my clothes fit well at least gives me some sense of being able to put my best foot forward.

> **"**
> WHO we see in the mirror reflects the physical, WHAT we see reflects the inner being that is our spiritual, mental, and emotional, Be willing to look beyond the surface.
> **"**

I have always looked in the mirror and found something noteworthy to say about myself. I refused to allow myself to see anything other than what is good. After all, isn't that what people with a healthy self-esteem do? We don't allow our vision to be marred by our negative opinion of ourselves, we refuse to see anything other than what's great and positive and uplifting when we look in the mirror. I would never allow myself to fall prey to the many people who expected me to be weak and pathetic because they looked at me with pity, disdain, or disgust due to my weight. I didn't see the pain of my past experiences or the self-inflicted trauma I've forced myself to endure. No, not me, never that, I looked in the mirror and saw the best of myself...I'm beautiful, I'm intelligent, I'm accomplished, I'm ambitious, I'm loved by my family and friends, and I'm pretty darn awesome. I'm.............

A liar! Plain and simple. Very rarely have I looked into mirrors and been able to say I am 100% happy with who or what I see looking backing at me. I looked at myself day in and day out pretending I was telling myself all these great truths, but I have never in my entire life believed them. I looked in the mirror and I didn't even recognize who I was. I told myself what I wanted to believe, I told myself what people expected me to believe. Why? I had spent my entire life hiding my weaknesses, my pain, and my shortcomings behind a wall. I had also spent many years being someone I was not. I conditioned myself to never show weakness, to never show that I needed someone, to ball all my hurt, disappointment, dreams, resentment, anger, and sadness into one huge ball of pain that I carried around with me day in and day out. That ball became the thing that beared me up and served as my foundational support and I was so afraid to let go of it for fear that if I did, I would break into a million fragments of fragile pieces that could never be whole again.

This defense mechanism was my way of dealing with the pain associated with living in an overweight body my entire life. The stigmatism and discrimination associated with obesity was a very real part of my existence. I struggled to find ways to make myself more likable, more acceptable, more lovable. I was the nice, kind, committed, hard worker. As a child, I can remember feeling that if I was all these things, my weight wouldn't matter. I went out of my way to be the good child, the model student, the helpful friend, and the dependable worker. But no matter what I did I was often treated as lazy, weak, unintelligent, and unworthy. As an adult, who has done the work to heal from past trauma, her own junk, and the perceptions and opinions of those around her, I have learned to seek that from my relationship with God, however, as a child, a teen, a young woman unsecure in her place in God, I sought it outwardly and felt a piece of me die every time my kindness was rewarded with hurtful, painful, action.

I can remember days of feeling the burden of my weight pressing me down into an abyss of hopelessness and despair and wishing someone, anyone, could see, understand, and help me with my pain. As I share my story with you now, I can think of so many occasions where I was just completely devastated in life because of being made to feel as if I was a burden because of my weight.
One of the times that stick out the most occurred during my first year of high school. I am a huge music fan, I love music of all types, and it has always been a source of joy and happiness for me. I loved

to listen to music from an early age. I am pretty sure this love was something I gained from my father, who I can remember always listening to music in some way throughout my childhood years. From playing it on Saturday mornings when we were cleaning and doing our chores, to blasting it when we were riding in his car, or when he was outside washing and cleaning it. From hearing him sing around the house and spontaneously burst into a dance when a song was really speaking to him, music was always something positive. I embraced this love of music that he shared with us and developed my own musical life journey; taking piano lessons at an early age, learning how to play the clarinet, joining the band in middle school, and then joining the marching band in high school.

I knew that my participation in the high school band would be extremely difficult as it would require a level of physical activity that was outside the scope of anything I had done before. It taxed me and challenged me even far beyond what I could imagine but I persevered and made the band after a very strenuous summer band camp and summer practice experience (Shout out to all my fellow summer band campers who completely understand the pain of marching, running drills, etc. in the hot summer heat all day for an entire week). I was so looking forward after the hard working summer to a year filled with football games, band competitions, traveling, and just having fun. All of that came screeching to a halt however as soon as it came time to be fitted for the band uniforms.

In most cases, bands don't order new uniforms every year as this can be costly and very expensive, so they recycle during the years when a new order is not being made. There is nothing wrong with this practice as it saves money and allows for members to be quickly fitted. For me however, it was an absolute nightmare, as they couldn't find a uniform for me to use because of my size. The band director and parent volunteers worked so hard to find a uniform that would fit but I was absolutely mortified when I was told that the only thing they could do for me was give me two uniforms so that I could try to find someone to alter them into one that might work. My mother diligently sought and found someone who could do this and the seamstress she found did her absolute best but of course the uniform never fit appropriately.

I would spend every Friday night game and every Saturday competition having to be pinned up so the pants wouldn't fall since they never came fully up to my waist. My mom would pin the bottom of the top to the waist of the pants in hopes that while I was marching my pants wouldn't fall and my top wouldn't rise and show all my business. I would agonize every performance worrying about what would happen if those pins popped. My stomach would be in knots and I would be sweating bullets so afraid to have another thing to draw attention to myself. In my mind, my weight was already enough! Sometimes a safety pin would come loose, and I would march an entire show or spend an entire game feeling it sticking into my skin and poking me through the material of the uniform. But I just remeber enduring it and suffering because I didn't want to make a spectacle of myself.

I would hear so many derogatory, hurtful comments from my band mates, their parents, community members and fans, whenever we performed. I could see people pointing and laughing whenever we marched by the stands and although I was crying inside, I just kept pushing forward and pretended not to see or hear them. Something that I had so much love for became something that was a source of heartache, embarrassment and another reminder of just how much my weight made me a laughingstock and how cruel people could really be to those who they identify as "different".

So, after only a year, I decided to never march again and devoted myself to just being the band "student manager" so I could still travel and enjoy the experience but never have to be "on display" in that uniform ever again. Big shout out to the greatest band director ever, Mr. Dwight McMillan! I can't even remember what I told him at the time about why I desired to quit. I am sure he probably realized the truth behind my request to switch roles, but he graciously allowed me to become his assistant. He never made me feel less than because of my decision and made sure I worked just as hard in my role as the other band students.

Looking back on that situation now, I can see how even then God was working to turn something that was a source of pain for me into something that worked for my good. In his infinite wisdom, during my time spent in this role, my gift and love for planning, organizing, and strategizing was birthed and those gifts have served me well throughout my professional career and even now as an entrepreneur and author.

> **"**
> Only God can transform the thing you see as a source of pain into something that will help birth your purpose.
> **"**

Again, this is just one example, the DAILY trauma of being picked on, insulted, overlooked, frowned upon, laughed at, and hurt meant I retreated into a world where I felt safe. In this world, I didn't have to open myself up to the potential of being wounded or disappointed. Thinking about it now, I can see again how even then strategically God allowed my pain to plant another seed of purpose. One of the things I did in this safe space I created for myself was explore the world through reading books. It was through reading that my desire to one day author my own books was birthed.

Although I can now look back on that time in my life and find the positive, it is so important for me to let you know once again that I am even now writing this book from a place where I am still healing. In this safe space I created for myself, I spent so much time focused on escaping that I ignored some hard-core truths that if faced earlier in life would have led me to understanding something very important: In order for us to shift ourselves into the position to fulfill the purpose and potential God imparted into our lives at birth, and see our dreams fulfilled, we have got to face the looking glass with 100% truth, put our big girl/big boy panties/underwear on and OWN OUR STUFF!

If we allow ourselves to shift beyond what we see physically when we look in the mirror and delve deeper, we can use what we see as a powerful tool. It can allow us to take an introspective look beyond the physical and see the mental and emotional parts of our inner beings that we have kept hidden from others but more importantly from ourselves. The mirror became a place for me to look past my imperfections and simply began to reflect and relax in the power of being me. Learning to do this meant being able to check-in with how I was really feeling about myself, my hurt, my pain, and my emotional trauma. I used the mirror to remove the mask and face myself!

Being able to take a complete look at those times in my life when I was at my worst emotionally, physically, spiritually, and mentally, required me to not only allow myself to acknowledge the pain, but also to pray about it, dissect it, heal from it, learn from it, and yes even use it. It also required me to recognize my own role in it. So, because I know how difficult this was for me, I'm going to go first. Here are the truths I've hidden for far too long from myself and from everyone who knows me. Here are the truths that I was forced to take ownership of before God ever imparted one word to put into this book and here are the truths, He told me I must be willing to share with you, to help you begin the process of walking through your own journey of healing and deliverance:

1. I am most ashamed of the fact that I have allowed myself to become a 51-year-old diabetic weighing almost 500 pounds. Writing this book and facing my own personal looking glass has allowed me to realize that all the fear, anger, resentment, hurt, pain, and sadness I thought were hidden deep within me, manifested themselves outwardly in the one area of my life I refused to control: my weight.

As mentioned earlier, I have spent my entire life being overweight. I don't know what it even means to be considered a normal sized person. I was a fat baby, a fat child, a fat teenager, and am now even still a fat woman. I'm not laying blame for my weight and lack of discipline in this area on anyone else but myself. I have never been strong enough to change it, and so I chose to ignore it because pretending to be the fake Verna that was okay with the world and lived in the land of rainbows and lollipops allowed me to ignore and neglect the reality of doing the hard work to be a healthier version of myself.

Notice I said healthier and not skinnier. My goal now as an adult grown woman is not so much about losing weight as it is about being a more healthy, productive me. When I was younger however, losing weight was all I heard about so I went out of my way to not think about it. I was a rebel with an insane cause. My mission was to never use my size as a crutch and to show everyone I could do anything I put my mind to no matter how much I weighed. I thought if I just did enough, people would leave me alone and I could have some peace. Things didn't always work out in my favor, but I wasn't going down without trying.

My weight became the one thing in my life I refused to control but in a twisted way, it also became the thing I obsessed over the most. At that time in my life though, I didn't recognize that was happening. I convinced myself not focusing on my size meant I was liberated, well adjusted, and proving a point to the world and to everyone who had teased me, insulted me, been rude to me, used me or ignored me. Because those very people oftentimes needed me and so I would put my Super Woman cape on and come to the rescue. Not realizing that all I was doing was adding more weight to my shoulders. Not only was I physically heavy, I was also emotionally heavy as well.

I have lived a lifetime of this foolishness, because as smart as I am, it never struck me that losing weight would probably have been so much easier!

2. I have wasted so much time pretending to be the person I thought people needed me to be, because I was afraid the person I was, would never be good enough. I became addicted to being needed because to me being needed by someone meant at some base level, they could overlook my weight and really accept me. I was Verna, the oldest daughter, the oldest grandchild, the oldest sister, the sweet girl, the responsible child, the loving aunt, the helpful friend, the overachiever, the organizer, the planner, the hard worker, the loyal one, the studious one, the dependable one, the strong one, the one who carried everyone's burdens, the fixer, the problem solver and the list goes on and on and on. All in the hopes that my weight would be overlooked, and I would be more lovable and likable. I just wanted to be enough so that my weight didn't matter.

This need to be needed for me became another unhealthy habit I should never have begun. It moved beyond the basic need of feeling significant and accepted into an unhealthy way for me to validate my own sense of self-worth. I was a consummate people-pleaser, ingratiating myself to others so that I could feel more loved, worthy of their time and attention, and appreciated outside of the scope of my size.

I felt like people needing me provided me a purpose and I felt empowered. The result of looking for my purpose outside of God, who is of course the one who ordains our purpose, was that I of course was unfulfilled and lost. By focusing so much on satisfying the

> **"**
> Your true purpose can only be found through an intentional, intimate, and consistent relationship with God.
> **"**

needs of others, I inadvertently also neglected my own needs. I learned at an early age to put me last and that trait has traveled with me throughout life. I spent too much of my time doing and not enough time being. This meant I often developed codependent relationships built upon the foundation of my insecurity. Because of this, they were never beneficial. I stayed in too many of those relationships far too long and it took much prayer, courage, and inner strength to end them.

3. I refused to share my entire self with any person I could potentially have a relationship with, friend or otherwise, because doing so had always resulted in pain. Responding to a perceived need allowed me to engage with others on my terms and control the flow of our relationship.

From an early age I associated love with pain. Imagine spending every day of your childhood feeling bullied, invisible, and misunderstood by some of the very people you admired, loved, and befriended. I didn't know how to

> **"**
> True love doesn't cause pain. People who have been hurt themselves cause pain for others.
> **"**

express how fragile my mental state was, couldn't verbalize

my pain, and was too afraid to share how often I considered hurting myself to end my suffering. Even the sanctity of my family was not a space where I felt like my feelings and my struggles would be understood.

The sad reality is that mistreating people who are overweight is such a norm for society that most people don't think twice about what they say or how they treat those who are considered overweight or obese. They simply see nothing wrong with their comments or their actions because of course, you can just always "stop eating and change it." Even when they are making the cruelest comments, they simply see it as trying to help. The thing some members of my family and friends never realized was that trying to help me by insulting me and drawing unnecessary attention only brought awareness to the fact that I was too weak to fix it and made me hate myself even more.

Now that I have grown and allowed myself to own my truth, it has become easier for me to begin to let go of the bad habits which contributed to my being obese. This is a daily battle requiring sometimes even more than I believe I can sacrifice to change it, but I have learned to lean on and depend on God for His guidance, strength, and grace as I work on becoming whole and well in order that I can fulfill His purpose for my life. You see, the reality is that when we operate and live at less than our best selves, we cannot fully sow into the lives we have been ordained by God to bless and impact.

While an integral part of my journey to healing, my weight

however is not meant to be the focus of this book. It is not meant to be a diary of my trials and struggles while growing up as the big kid, who became a bigger teen, and who then became an even bigger adult. It is not about being so large you know those around you "see" you but yet you feel invisible everywhere you go. It is not about being a little girl who craved validity and acceptance from those around her but was made to feel as if she never really belonged anywhere. It is not about trying so hard to be a "good girl" because being BIG seemed to be enough trouble for everyone to deal with. It is not about being ridiculed, laughed at, embarrassed, left out, hurt, insulted, used by those you thought cared, shunned, or being disliked solely because you have the audacity to expect better.

This book is about my absolute fervent desire to own every fiber of who I am at every stage in this journey called life and LIVE BIG (Bold, Inspired, Gifted). I have devoted myself to doing whatever it takes to shift from BEING big to LIVING BIG (Bold, Inspired, Gifted) every day. My dream is that in sharing my process with you, that you will begin your own journey to living BIG and in doing so chase after and realize your dreams! Living BIG is not just about the physical you, but also about the mental, emotional, and spiritual you as well.

It involves owning every bit of who you are and pouring out ALL of what God has placed in you to leave a footprint on the world that impacts, inspires, and encourages others to do the same.

> **"** Living BIG is not just about the physical, but also about the mental, emotional, and spiritual you as well. **"**

Prayer #1: Heavenly Father, I believe

in your power and pray that as I begin this process of stepping outside of my comfort zone to live a bold, inspired, and gifted life, you would help me to have the vision to see the real me. Be my strength when I am weak and give me courage when I am afraid. I surrender myself to this process and believe God that you will honor my commitment. Please walk with me, guide me, and speak to me so that I can fulfill your purpose for my life. I trust you; I honor you and I love you. In your precious name I pray, Amen.

BIG Step #1: Allow yourself at least thirty (30) minutes or more to complete this step. Find the biggest mirror you have in your home. Close your eyes, take a few relaxing breaths, open your eyes, and honestly tell yourself who you see. Take a good long look and really evaluate who you are. Look beyond just the physical and see your spiritual, mental, and emotional self as well. Do not be afraid to see all of you, the good, the bad, and the ugly. All those things make up the sum total of who we ALL are. You are not alone. There are no perfect people! We are all striving every day to be better versions of who we were yesterday. Spend time getting to know the you, you've failed to allow yourself to see. Take off the mask and look deeply into the rawness of every scar, emotion, fear, strength, gift, and desire. Do not leave the mirror until you have taken a deep look into all the things that make you... YOU!

I am a huge fan of journals, the prettier and more unique they are, the better, so in this book there is a scripted journal entry following every chapter. Grab your Living BIG journal and your favorite pen and let's "Get Our Journal On."

Journal Entry #1: Who do I see in the mirror? What things have I hidden from myself? What things have I hidden form others? What events, people, and circumstances have framed the way I view myself? What would I like to see when I look in the mirror that I don't see now? Is that person already there and I just refuse to see them? Why? How can that person begin to show up daily?

Chapter Two

BIG Reality: Who Am I?
BEING THE BEST YOU, YOU CAN BE, NOT THE
YOU OTHERS EXPECT YOU TO BE.

Completing BIG Step #1 was super hard for me and it took more than one time "looking" in the mirror to see beyond just the physical into my spiritual, mental, and emotional self as well. What I learned through that time though was that I hadn't ever taken the time to see beyond the surface of who I thought I was. I saw flaws and imperfections, I saw who I convinced myself I was, and who others might even think I was, I saw some good things and some bad things. I saw things I admired and things I despised. However, staying there long enough to see "beyond what I saw" was a painful but necessary process. It was through this process, that I began to see the hidden things!

The process involves coming to understand that even what you perceive as weaknesses or flaws can be used as gifts to transform your life and the life of others. It meant beginning to deal with my deepest most innermost thoughts and actions. It meant acknowledging that I was emotionally wounded. In a sense, by living the way I was, I was not only ignoring the emotional trauma I had experienced, but I also became my own abuser. I had disregarded my feelings and in doing so had given myself permission to say that my pain wasn't important. I thought I should be stronger, less emotional, less sensitive, able to overcome the comments, the teasing, the bullying, and so I refused to deal with the fact that I couldn't deal with it, I didn't know how.

By suppressing my pain, I had become angry, unhappy, felt hopeless and powerless, unworthy, and broken. Albert Einstein once said, "You cannot solve a problem with the same mind that created it." The more time I spent in that mirror, the more I realized that some things had to change. Yet I also realized I didn't have the capacity or knowledge of how to begin changing them. I mean after all, I had been pretending they didn't exist for many years. I looked at myself and acknowledged that I felt defeated and like a fraud. I was emotionally drained and had no desire to live at all, much less live BIG. I was over myself, over trying, and I was overwhelmed.

> **"**
> I had disregarded my feelings and in doing so had given myself permission to say that my pain wasn't important.
> **"**

But it was here, in my most broken state, that I felt God speak to me through his word.

"For of this I am confident, that He who has begun a good work within you will go on to perfect it in preparation for the day of Jesus Christ" - Philippians 1:6

"I shall not die, but love, and tell of the works of the Lord" - Psalm 118:17

The most amazing thing about God is that He isn't selfish and what He does for one of His children He can do for all. This same God who helped me shift beyond my place of despair, can and will do it for you also. Once I was 100% honest about who I saw in the mirror, not what others saw or what I pretended to be, it opened the door for God to reveal what He saw. The most critical part of this journey for me has been connecting to God as my Creator to know who HE designed me to be. In Psalms, 139:14 of the Bible, David pens the words, "I praise you for I am fearfully and wonderfully made…" No matter what YOU see through your own eyes, remember in God's eyes you are amazing! He made you in His image! I had to begin to see myself through His eyes because MY vision was flawed. His vision helped me to understand that He loved me despite my imperfections.

It is imperative that you allow yourself to know who you are in Him, so you can fully live your life the way He intended and fulfill your God-given destiny and purpose. To do this, it means really taking the time to know GOD. Once you know who He is, then it will be easier for you to know yourself and live a life that reflects HIS vision of you to the world. Simply put, the opinion of others doesn't matter and neither does yours. God's opinion is the only one that matters when it comes to your identity and purpose because He created you. The most reliable source for knowing God and understanding how precious we are to him is of the course the Bible.

In His word, we are told some fundamental truths about who we are in God: we are new creations (II Corinthians 5:18), we are loved

(I John 3:3), we are His children (Galatians 3:26), we are joint heirs, we have a Godley legacy (Romans 8:17), we are made complete through His son Jesus (Colossians 2:10), and we are chosen, Holy, and loved (Colossians 3:12).

> **"**
> God's opinion is the only one that matters when it comes to your identity and purpose because He created you.
> **"**

The more time I spent in His word, the more I realized that I wasn't living up to my potential as His daughter. I was living beneath my privilege. I knew that I had to really break old habits by looking outside of my own vision and searching within myself by connecting to the Creator who is the source of all healing, forgiveness, wisdom, and power. This process became the preparation I needed to begin to truly live life in a BIG way. I began to understand through time spent with God that the process of changing the things I didn't like when I looked in the mirror had to begin with prayer and time spent getting to know Him more intimately. There is no you without God. The Creator formed you and knew you even before you were born. You have been predestined for a purpose and it is time to be BIG enough to walk into that destiny. The Kingdom has need of your gifts!

Will this be easy? Heck no! For as much as God desires you to be ALL He created you to be, there will be obstacles, trials, non-supporters, naysayers, backstabbers, even YOU will at times sabotage the work God is trying to do in your life. What I can surely say has worked for me is in the toughest of times, God reminds me that I am His, that He is the compass, and He will direct my path. Seeing through the lens of God's love meant recognizing that the "me" I see, or others see doesn't matter, only the "me" God sees is important. It doesn't mean I overlook areas I need to correct or work on; it means committing myself to doing the work to change it and grow.

This work must begin with one thing: obedience. One of the most tangible aspects of our love for God is our obedience to Him. For you to shift forward into BIG living you must hear and obey God's voice. Cultivating a spirit of obedience has been the game changer for me! I obey even when I'm afraid to because living BIG means you must be bold enough to take the leaps and walk off the mountains and do things differently than you ever have before because you know God's got you! He won't ever let you fall and even if you stumble, He is always there to pick you up and set you back on the right path. I've fallen and gotten things wrong more times than I can even count, but I know without a doubt, God has never left me. He believed in me even when I didn't believe in myself.

His faith in me meant His pushing me to finish this book that he inspired me to begin over eight years ago. Despite my fear, uncertainty, insecurity, and disobedience, He kept speaking to me. He kept inspiring me. He kept taking me through this process, step by step, over and over, until He knew for sure I had finally reached a place where I was ready to complete it. I was a poor student, often having to repeat most steps in this process several times, but God never gave up on me. As I stated before, I am still growing and learning, but I am committed to the process and that has made all the difference.

Prayer #2: Father God as I continue this journey, open my eyes, uncloud my vison, and help me to see myself through your eyes. I thank you for creating me in your image and for never leaving me or forsaking me despite my own self-sabotage, self-preservation tactics, or disobedience. Forgive me for times when I haven't listened to your directions or when I convinced myself that I wasn't worthy of your love and attention. I commit myself to spending quality time with you so that I can clearly hear your voice. Guide me, direct me, and lead me in the path that you would have me to go. Help me continue to gain knowledge of your love for me, so that I can be more loving of myself and be able to share my true self with those around me. In your precious name I pray, Amen.

Big Step #2: Take a blank sheet of paper and fold it into half, then fold it over again. You should have four equal parts which we will call quadrant 1, 2 3, and 4. Label the quadrants as follows:

Quadrant #1 – Who Do I Say I Am?

Quadrant #2 – Who Does God Say I Am?

Quadrant #3 – How Can I Maximize My Strengths?

Quadrant #4 – What Ares Do I Need to Improve?

For this BIG STEP, please fill out the top two sections completely: Who Do I Say I Am? and Who Does God Say I Am? You will fill out the bottom two sections after reading the next chapter.

Journal Entry #2: What are the differences and similarities in how I see myself and how God sees me? What things can I commit to doing daily to see myself more as God sees me? What are some barriers that I may encounter? How can I break through them? In what areas does my obedience need to grow?

Chapter Three

BIG Shift: Navigating Strengths and Shortcomings
EMBRACING THE POSITIVES AND CHANGING THE NEGATIVES

To be able to embrace both the positives and negatives that you experience throughout life, you must be able to adopt a mindset that allows you to balance negative and positive thinking in a way that allows for you to thrive. Notice that I said balance and not get rid of. The reality is that no matter where you are in life, you will always experience negativity in some form or fashion. And no, it won't always come from other people, even you will still have negative thoughts. Living a positive life does not mean your life is 100% void of anything negative. The negative however can be transformed by taking the time to identify the source and creating a positive mindset that allows you to not only recognize it but also embrace it, modify it, and grow from it.

Mindset determines how we fell about ourselves and about the things we experience. It can control our thoughts, emotions, and behaviors in any given situation. In her 2007 book, Mindset, Stanford psychologist Carol Dweck states that it is not intelligence, talent, or education that sets successful people apart, but it is their mindset and how they approach life's challenges. She identifies two basic mindsets: fixed and growth.

A fixed mindset means you believe your abilities cannot be changed and your talents, and intelligence alone lead to your achievement. A growth mindset on the other hand means you believe that you talents and abilities can be developed over time through effort and persistence.

> **"** It is not intelligence, talent, or education that sets successful people apart, but it is their mindset and how they approach life's challenges. -Carol Dweck **"**

Embracing a growth mindset, I believe is integral to this journey of living life in a bolder, more inspired, and more gifted way. If you don't believe you can change, you won't. Being able to see trials, pain, and trauma in your life as an opportunity to learn, grow, and overcome obstacles can help you to shift your perspective. Dweck also provided four ways to shift from fixed mindset to a growth mindset:

1. *Listen to yourself and use thought awareness to combat negative thinking.* Challenge any negative thoughts by stating the exact opposite and recognizing why those positive thoughts are truth.

2. *Recognize that you have a choice.* We all have barriers, obstacles, and challenges. It is how you respond to them that matters. Use them for your good by developing plans of actions to equip to navigate and overcome them.

3. *Challenge your fixed mindset.* No matter how inadequate you feel, remember in this world we live in, there is ALWAYS a way for you to learn new skills and better prepare yourself to achieve your goals. Allow yourself to room to not only expand your mind and grow but also to fail forward and try as many times as it takes to succeed.

4. *Take action.* Be proactive about shifting your mindset to

tackle obstacles. Will Smith once said, "At the center of bringing any dream into fruition is self-discipline." We must discipline our minds to take the action it needs to allow us to grow and become everything our hearts desire."

This discipline is critical to overcoming our own self-doubt. At some point in all our lives, we have felt inferior or not good enough either through our own feelings of inadequacy or through the actions of someone around us. Getting over our own negative self-doubt is tough. So is getting over the toxic negativity we have allowed into our lives via unhealthy relationships we've developed and kept with the people around us. While identifying what others have done to contribute to our inferiority complex is probably easy, it is much harder however to identify when we are the source of our own issues. As cliché' as it might sound, walking through this journey of healing has shined a huge magnifying glass on the fact that I have been and am now even in some ways my greatest enemy.

I had allowed myself to fall prey to the belief that I wasn't good enough. I always wanted to be someone other than who God made me to be. I constantly felt inferior to those around me and cannot even begin to tell you how much anxiety I felt from worrying about being less than. Because of this negative perception, it seemed as if no matter how hard I worked that there was never a time when I could positively say I was proud of myself. I was in a constant state of trying to find ways to be happier and more self-assured. Lately, I have realized that I only deceived myself into believing that I had joy. You know the kind of joy we sing about, that unspeakable joy that isn't shaken by situation or circumstance? Yeah, I spent years of my life pretending I had it only to realize I didn't even know what it truly was.

It has taken me a long time to find it and I now know that even when I thought I had it, I never fully experienced it until recently! You see it is so very different from just being happy. Happy is conditional while joy is not! Happy says I feel good in the moment, joy says I am determined to feel good ALWAYS! It didn't come from people, things, or achievements, it came from spending time with God and realizing that joy is a "gift" from Him. It is available to all of us but the deep residual contentment and peace that joy brings can only be found through spending time with Him. We serve a God who is mighty, awesome, and amazing and in Him I am beautiful, wonderful, accomplished, satisfied, and loved beyond what I can sometimes even comprehend.

In Him I can live BIG (Bold, Inspired, and Gifted) every day and so can you!

> **"** True joy is a gift from God! It is available to all of us but the deep residual contentment and peace that joy brings can only be found through spending time with Him. **"**

Until we begin to really see ourselves as a valuable human being not because of what we do or don't do but just because God created us, we cannot understand how to prevent our shortcomings from becoming a consuming cloud of doubt and fear which paralyzes us and keeps us from living our best lives! We must cultivate a practice of seeing the positives about ourselves first before we chip away at our confidence by focusing on the negatives. Being able to face life's ups, downs, twists, and challenges with a positive outlook will determine how successful you will be at moving forward beyond your hurt, pain, and past trauma. I too had to shift my perspective and learn how to do this.

Feelings of inadequacy began at an early age. I remember always being talked about or noticed in most cases because of my weight. As expressed in earlier chapters, many people around me made derogatory comments, called me unpleasant names, and focused negatively on my weight no matter what I did or achieved. Once I started my own journey of transformation however, I came to believe that at times their intent might have been to be helpful, and their comments were given as a form of tough love. However, the sting of constantly being the focus of negative attention because of my weight, meant I spent much of my childhood in a constant state of emotional pain.

As a young girl, I didn't know how to deal with the ugly comments and the ugly things that were done to me because of my weight. As shared in Chapter Two, for this reason, I began to build a shell of protection around me that I have only in recent years begun to allow myself to chip away at. The shell for me was my protective gear. It was a wall that was built up every time I was hurt, afraid, doubted, deceived, made to feel not good enough, used or betrayed. It grew every time I lied to myself and others about who I was, what I felt, what I needed, and what I allowed myself to become. In this shell, I hardened my heart against the mental abuse and bullying. I dealt with it in ways that became the self-preservation landscape by which I lived my life. But it hindered me so much more than it helped me.

By closing myself off from the world emotionally, I felt I was protecting myself from being further scarred by the people in my life who had caused me so much pain. All of this was going on inside me but to the outside world I pretended to be the same Verna that most people thought they knew. I was still being kind, helping others, giving of myself, supporting, loving, and doing, but I was dying inside. I am sure you like me have your very own list of these types of hurts and emotional scarring. I can honestly share with you however that you CAN like me, also turn your pain into purpose and power.

Once I began to really take a deep dive into all that makes me who I am, I also realized that as I grew older, in order to protect myself from being hurt and taken advantage of, I had also become angry, defensive, untrusting, overbearing, abrasive, and impatient. This was not an easy pill to swallow as I had always tried to be nice.

I mean this was one of my strategies to overcome the stigmatism associated with being overweight and the negative mistreatment; to be nice and kind to everyone in hopes that they MIGHT be nice and kind to me.

> " You can turn your pain into your purpose and power. "

When some of my interactions and engagements with those around me led to my being told that I was hard to work for and with, not nice, self-centered, stubborn, and aggressive, I was at first in disbelief. I worked so hard to be the exact opposite of those things, but what I didn't realize at the time was that despite my best efforts, those things that I thought were buried deep down inside of me, had begun to seep out and permeate the atmosphere around me. In so many ways, I was dead inside. Just as a dead body is hard and begins to stink if left attended, my heart had become hardened and the things that I refused to deal with emotionally, mentally, and physically began to stink up my thoughts, words, and actions. And just as a dead body begins to decompose after a certain amount of time, I knew that if left uncorrected, my life would begin to fall apart and crumble right before my eyes.

In the motion picture of my life, I was busy playing the role of the victim, however, I didn't read the full manuscript. I missed several critical parts of the movie! I had allowed the pain, hurt, and disappointments of those who "did me wrong" to fester inside and it was slowly eating me alive. It was so much easier to bury the hurt than deal with it and to confront it head on. The desire to be accepted far outweighed the need to handle improper behavior so I became a pro at pushing the pain aside so I could move beyond it. I told myself that by ignoring the pain, I was rising above it. But I was so very wrong. By ignoring it, I allowed it to begin to darken my heart and desstroy my soul. I became bitter.

Bitterness is the result of hanging onto our emotional hurt and pain instead of going through the process which allows us to heal from it and move beyond it. The horrible thing about bitterness is that it takes up residence in and then overtakes our hearts. I allowed myself to bury my emotional pain because in essence I did not know what to do to make it go away. I felt powerless to control my weight and angry all the time. Although I was angry with people who hurt me and rightfully so, I learned though the healing process that I was most angry with myself. I also learned that there are times when our pain can be very real but there are also times when our pain can be imagined.

For example, we can feel wounded by something we "think" someone said or did and without even confirming it, our imagination gets the best of us, and we get carried away by a speculation that might not even be true. Be very careful that the root of your bitterness isn't growing from

> **"**
> The horrible thing about bitterness is that it takes up residence in and then overtakes our hearts.
> **"**

false assumptions. If you aren't clear about someone's inner motivations or a situation, be mature enough to ask and gain clarity. Learning how to do this has saved me from adding weight to the load of suffering that I was already walking through healing from.

Bitterness was also the thing that crushed my ability to truly experience God's joy.

"Let all bitterness, and wrath, and anger, and clamor, and evil speaking, be put away from you, with all malice: And be ye kind one to another, tenderhearted, forgiving one another, even as God for Christ's sake hath forgiven you." - Ephesians 4:31-32

Breaking the chain of bitterness means choosing to change the way you process your pain. It is so easy to just be stuck in resentment over past hurt and unfair treatment. Sadly, it is just as easy to become the kind of person who harbors resentment, and that resentment begins to transition into bitterness that we can't heal from because we have become comfortable with it. The bitterness becomes a badge of honor or a cloak we carry on our backs. It is our way of saying to the world, "Look at me, over here, I am hurt, I am broken, I am in need of healing." It provides a way for us to be relevant when we feel we are irrelevant and unseen.

The danger in doing this is that when we don't operate from a true desire to overcome, learn from, and use our pain for the greater good, we fall prey to the habit of broadcasting and bringing attention to our pain only to use it to make ourselves matter. In addition, this refusal to heal oftentimes is because we become addicted to the energy, confidence, and boost we get from living in righteous indignation. That feels way better than having to deal with the vulnerability of exposing our self-doubt.

It is possible however to break the bonds of bitterness that exist in your life. There is a story in the Bible about a woman named Naomi. In the book of Ruth, we are introduced to Naomi and learn that she lost both her husband and two sons. Amid considering what she and her two daughters-in-law would do she decided to transition them from Moab to Belen to seek out food because there was a famine in the earth. During this time, Naomi asks her two daughters-in-law to leave her because she was frustrated and sad because she could not provide for them and had nothing to give them. One of them leaves and one decides to stay with her. In the text, we learn that Naomi decides to change her name. ""Don't call me Naomi, she told them. Call me Mara because the Almighty has made my life very bitter." Ruth 1:20

Like Naomi, I have found myself feeling justifiable pain and suffering but not knowing how to manage them or handle them without God's input and guidance. Bitter people often never feel gratitude because they spend so much time focused on what is going wrong. Like Naomi we can't see beyond our circumstances. Naomi focused on what was lost but not on what was gained. She bemoaned the fact she had lost her husband, sons, and one daughter in law but did not appreciate the fact that she still had the affection and loyalty of her daughter-in-law Ruth.

When we operate in a spirit of bitterness, we also often don't want to accept help or consider that others may support us. Like Naomi we push away the people who want to be there during our hard times, and we neglect to thank God for the help He does provide for us. The help that we sometimes are too blind to see. When we are bitter, we thrive on adopting a victim mentality and look at our circumstances and not the God who can deliver us from them. We become passive and feel as if we aren't in control. The good news though is that God has a way of turning our bitter into better.

No matter how grim our situation may seem, I know that God can turn it around. I can testify that this is true because He has done it for me, and He will also do it for you. Although Naomi operated from a place of bitterness, God didn't allow her to stay there, and the end of her story was very different from the beginning. God used other people to remind her of His love and in doing so, she regained her happiness and developed an attitude of gratitude. "The women said to Naomi: "Praise be to the Lord,

> ❝
> When we are bitter, we thrive on adopting a victim mentality and look at our circumstances and not the God who can deliver us from them.
> ❞

who this day has not left you without a guardian-redeemer (...) for your daughter in law, who loves you, has given him birth (...) Then Naomi took the child in her arms and cared for him" Ruth 4:14-16.

There is so much to unpack in this story, and I have also left out some other key details about how God changed Naomi's circumstances, so I encourage you to read the Book of Ruth in its entirety for yourself. The key point I want to share is that no matter how hard things seem for us and no matter how deep the root of bitterness has grown, there is a way out. But the path to releasing its hold will truly be a journey you need to walk one step at a time.

Take control of the bitterness in your life by resolving every day to find reasons to be thankful and grateful. Find purpose in your pain and don't allow your pain to cripple or destroy you. You are stronger, mightier, and more blessed than you even know and God and His entire army has your back! Remember that we have been given the ability to create our own realities. We can choose to manage our emotional pain in a way that allows us to become better versions of ourselves. Managing the pain involves acknowledging it, praying about it, healing through it, and learning from it.

Acknowledgement

The weird thing about acknowledging pain is that when we hurt, we know it right? We can feel it but feeling it and allowing yourself to acknowledge it exists are two very different things. When we feel the hurt, we just want it to go away and so we mentally begin to war with how we can purge it mentally, physically, and emotionally. For example, if we have a cut, we apply pressure, find some ointment, and put a band-aid on it. Some of us, however, get hurt and do our best to ignore the pain oftentimes to our detriment. I'm one of those people, and it was easier for me to ignore the impact of the pain I experienced and just simply bury it.

Unfortunately, refusing to deal with our emotional pain leads us straight into emotional conflict. In essence we create a vacuum of negative imbalance. For example, all the years that I spent suppressing my pain, I can remember always feeling as if something was just "off" in my life. No matter how "happy" the things I experienced or accomplishments I achieved made me feel, I always felt like I was never living up to my full potential and was constantly seeking outside resources to fix whatever the "off" feeling was. I recognize now that this was self-destructive behavior.

Emotional pain can show up in different ways, it can be an uncomfortable physical reaction to an action or event, or it could be a sense of feeling emotionally overwhelmed. To begin the healing process, I had to learn how to allow myself to take the time to acknowledge the impact of the emotional trauma I experienced. Acknowledgement just simply means allowing yourself to recognize that you do actually "feel" something. Whether it be anger, sadness, anguish, or something else entirely, you have some type of response to it. Sometimes you may not be able to even recognize or identify what you feel exactly and that is fine.

Give yourself permission to be okay with knowing that something happened which negatively impacted you. Also be honest enough with yourself to ascertain the source of what you feel. Was it a result of your own actions or was it because of something that wasn't your fault? Recognizing the source is important. If you are the source, what behavior modifications or amends do you need to make to move toward resolving things and begin the healing process. Recognize when you are doing things that are self-destructive.

> " Allow yourself time to acknowledge the impact of the emotional trauma you experience. "

Self-destructive behaviors are those that harm you in some way physically, mentally, or emotionally. No matter who you are, you will at one point in your life or another do something that could be considered self-destructive. It's perfectly okay, we've all been there before. I strongly encourage you to pause for a minute and really consider the ways in which you have intentionally and unintentionally been the source of your own emotional pain.

Take it from the girl who has spent much of her life engaging in behaviors that were self-destructive, no matter how difficult it may seem, you can overcome them and change the things that you are doing to harm yourself. But the first thing you must do is be willing to admit them and acknowledge them. In many cases, our self-destructive behaviors are not intentional and in some cases they are.

Either way, the path to overcoming them can be as simple as making a conscious decision to change them, or in some cases being able to recognize that you may need assistance from friends or family members, or even in more critical cases, seek out therapy or counseling. Please know that there is no dishonor in seeking help to change the self-destructive behaviors you have identified. In the words of world

> **❝**
> Ask for help not because you're weak, but because you want to remain strong.
> - Les Brown
> **❞**

renowned motivational speaker, Les Brown, "Ask for help not because you're weak, but because you want to remain strong."

If you are like me though, there were also times when you quickly found a way to blame yourself for the actions of others as well. I can remember many times when I was wounded by others, and I somehow rationalized it by finding a way to make it my issue. For example, if I lost weight, perhaps the hurtful insults would not happen. Since I couldn't or wouldn't do the work to lose weight, I then deserved whatever people said about me. What I know now that I didn't know then, is how much more pain I inflicted on myself because of this type of thinking. Without even realizing it, I was adding to the mountain of emotional trauma I was already experiencing.

When you have been hurt by the actions of those around you, it is not your fault. Just like you have acknowledged and own up to doing things to hurt yourself, the people in your life who hurt you, must also own up to and acknowledge their role in your pain. This can be a daunting task especially for those of us who want to avoid anything that could potentially lead to conflict. Sometimes just a simple conversation with them helps them to see the error of their ways and they can modify their actions and you can move forward to building a healthier relationship.

In other times though, when dealing with those who refuse to accept their role in your pain, you may have to take a step back both from the situations that expose you to their actions or from the person by ending the relationship. Understanding that hurt people hurt people may allow you to move past their actions, however, you are responsible for protecting yourself from future trauma. What you are not responsible for doing is exposing yourself to anyone or anything that is a continued source of pain in your life.

When a cycle of hurtful behavior exists, you must do what it takes to break the cycle. By beginning to allow myself to acknowledge that my pain existed, I began to understand that whatever I felt as a result was valid and real. If I wanted to cry, I cried about it. If I wanted to scream, I screamed.

Acknowledging the hurt meant freeing myself to be unashamed about it and this was essential to my being able to step forward into healing from it. The reality is that when you are wounded and don't take the steps to allow God to heal you, those wounds can destroy you, your relationships, your career, and yes even your future.

> 66
> Protect yourself from future trauma. You are not responsible for exposing yourself to anyone or anything that is a continued source of pain in your life.
> 99

Prayer and Healing

I think for many people, another knee jerk reaction to being hurt by others is to attempt to fight back and hurt them in return. I can admit to having had many of those moments myself over the years. I will even admit to indulging this urge on many occasions. If I am being completely honest, I will even say that there were times when doing so was extremely satisfying. However, whether I indulged or ignored the urge to get revenge, the reality was that without fail, the pain and trauma went nowhere. It was with me as I rationalized fighting back, it was with me when I convinced myself fighting back wasn't worth it, and it was with me when I simply chose to ignore the pain existed. When God began to reveal how deeply my life had been impacted by the events and incidences which caused me pain, He also helped me to understand that the only path to healing from it began and ended with Him.

Whether the source of your emotional trauma is internal or external, you can heal from it. If the source is internal, the path to healing begins with repentance. Externally, when someone has hurt you physically, emotionally, or mentally, the path to healing begins with forgiveness. Remember when I wrote earlier about how we create emotional conflict when we ignore our emotional pain. This is when we begin to self-inflict emotional trauma onto ourselves. When we suppress our pain, we begin to allow anger, unforgiveness, bitterness, guilt, and self-doubt to fester in our hearts and minds. The only way to deal with this is through God's word and His presence in our lives. This begins with prayer and continues by immersing ourselves into the Word of God to learn what He has promised us as His children. We can be transformed by tapping into who He is and who He has created to us be.

Transformation however can only happen when there is a

renewing of our minds.

"And be not conformed to this world: but be ye transformed by the renewing of your mind, that ye may prove what is that good, and acceptable, and perfect, will of God." - Romans 12:2

To do this, we must learn how to replace the hurt and pain we feel with the power, love, and strength that comes through building a relationship with God. When we allow Him to show us who we are in Him and our views begin to line up with His, He begins to heal the deep wounds we have allowed to negatively impact our lives. When we let go of the discouragement, pain, and hurt, He will renew our thinking and give us a new vision for our lives.

The Word of God tells us in Deuteronomy 31:6 to "Be strong and of a good courage, fear not, nor be afraid of them: for the Lord thy God, he it is that doth go with thee; he will not fail thee, nor forsake thee". The most amazing thing God shared with me throughout this process is that He will never give up on me! He wants to restore our joy and be prosperous in every area of our lives.

"For I know the thoughts that I think toward you, saith the Lord, thoughts of peace, and not of evil, to give you an expected end."
- Jeremiah 29:11

Prayer allows us a safe space where we can share freely and openly how our emotional trauma affects and impacts us and those around us. This was hard for me to do because I felt like a failure and did not want to disappoint God with my weakness but then He gently reminded me that He knows everything about me so that nothing I could say to Him in prayer was a surprise. He is a compassionate, loving, and faithful Father who is always waiting to hear from us. If we don't express our pain to Him, we don't make room for Him to give us the revelation we need to heal and grow from it. Opening ourselves up to revealing and exploring the pain paves the road toward hearing God's voice to gain clarity and direction. This does not happen however without making the steps to connect with God through prayer. I think sometimes we don't pray because we have been taught that prayer must be some deep, grandiloquent soliloquy to connect with our Father.

It doesn't have to be, please know that our Father loves just having simple conversation with you. Of course, He is to be honored and revered but He is also a God who is approachable, loving, and who desire to hear from us. Prayer is simply talking and emptying out your heart to a God who is always listening. Pray with your heart and speak your real thoughts to God, be 100% authentic and truthful. He calls us to pray so we can fellowship with Him and connect to His presence in our lives. Prayer can be a powerful tool in our journeys to living BIG, remember to use it as much as needed as you work toward being bolder, living more inspired, and walking fully in your giftedness.

> **"** Opening ourselves up to revealing and exploring our pain paves the road toward hearing God's voice to gain clarity and direction. **"**

Learning

Pain in any form is not uncommon. No matter who you are, you will experience some form of pain at some point in your life. In most cases, pain is not something that we desire or embrace. When we experience it, our immediate response is to attempt to fix it, escape from it, or ignore it. I have learned however that if we can work through the process of assessing the source of the pain, working through the pain, and realizing the life lessons that may be attached to it, then we can use our emotional pain to our benefit.

Even though pain in some form is inevitable, the suffering that results from it doesn't have to be debilitating. One way to prevent this is to shift your perspective on your pain although the impact of pain can sometimes be overwhelming especially when you've been blindsided and hurt by those you love the most. Finding a way to focus on the positive aspects of the situation though, while I know extremely difficult, will open the door to our tapping into our inner strength and provide the courage we need to overcome the impact and residual effect of the emotional trauma we experience. The main way we can do this is to ask ourselves what specifically the action or situation could be showing us about ourselves and our own behaviors. We have to move beyond fixating on what's been done to us and instead focus on what we've done to ourselves.

As a young woman, I can remember having the opportunity to pour my gifts and talents into a community organization I truly believed in and wanted to help grow. I spent countless hours as a volunteer researching funding sources, drafting grant proposals, helping to strategically organize and structure the organization to maximize its community impact and launch several successful new community initiatives. After quite some time working with them, an opportunity to advance the work I was doing presented itself in the form of an open leadership position within the organization. I expressed an interest and was so excited about being able to expand the work I was doing in an even greater capacity. However, not only was I not considered for the position, I was also asked to assist the person who was named Director and was later told it was in large part due to their public image, connections, and educational background. In essence, the tireless work and commitment to the mission of the organization I had displayed meant nothing. I was great to be the work horse but not good enough to be considered for a leadership role.

Unfortunately, this had not been the first time I had sown my gifts and been committed and totally dedicated to something but been completely overlooked when the opportunity for advancement or recognition was presented. In each case, what was obviously clear to me was that my size prohibited me from being seen as someone who could be placed into a leadership position. Many studies have shown that as an overweight person, there is a stigma attached to obesity which often means that you are seen as having less leadership potential and the capacity to be taken less seriously or be more successful. Sadly, I can remember so many times in my life when this was obviously the case. Every time it happened, I was mortally wounded and emotionally traumatized. Because I was gravely wounded it was so easy for me to focus on the hurt and what was done to me.

It was only through God leading me to take these steps and work through this process toward Living BIG that I was challenged about my reasoning for continuing to place myself in the type of situations that would lead to this pain. The easy response was that I loved helping, I was a hard worker and when I committed myself to something I gave it 100% of me. My greatest desire was to let me work, my gifts, my dedication, and my loyalty just be enough to be more accepted and liked by people and that would mean my weight would be overlooked but of course it never was. However, God helped me see also that I had a "need to be needed" and that I oftentimes volunteered myself to be the "savior" in situations, jumping feet first and totally absorbing myself expecting nothing in return and then being wounded when I felt it wasn't appreciated or valued. This was a very hard reality for me to face. But once I allowed myself to really accept it, I was able to see ways that my emotional trauma could work to provide some valuable lessons to remember as I continued the pathway toward healing.

Pain allows us to identify who we are and why that matters.
Pain has a way of stripping down the insignificant and immaterial things in life that don't matter by making us spend our time and

attention on the things that really do, our heart and soul. It was through my pain that God helped me connect to the certainty of my own humanness. I had to stop pretending I didn't hurt and embrace the fact that as a living breathing being, I DID feel and that I was impacted. No matter how much I pretended to be unfazed by the hurtful things, I was wounded and emotionally scarred in a big way. But, if we are open to it, our pain can become a way for us to share our experiences with the world. Our pain then begins to pave the way to our purpose. There are people you know and people you haven't met yet who need to hear about your emotional trauma and how you are working to overcome it. Your story will help them write and rewrite their own stories of triumph.

Pain can provide insight into your strengths and weaknesses.
It forced me to tap into a strength that I didn't even realize I possessed and weaknesses I did not want to deal with. This self-awareness became a catalyst for rebuilding my self-esteem and sparked significant growth for me personally. I was forced to develop a deeper sense of self to promote the inner growth I needed to shift forward into walking in purpose. I had to spend time truly reflecting on connecting with my inner self. You must slow down and stop running from your pain long enough to spend time with yourself and with God.

Pain can help you be more resilient.
That time spent in reflection exposed areas in my life that I had previously not wanted to examine which toughened me up and built up my ability to withstand storms and be a braver more courageous version of myself. When you look back over all

you've lived through and endured, be sure you focus on the fact that YOU SURVIVED! No matter how painful, how hurtful, how traumatizing, how difficult it was, you are still here. Every day that you are here presents another opportunity for you to then rise above it, overcome it, and use it for your own good!

Pain can help us establish meaningful relationships.
Pain doesn't leave room for our ego and pride, rather it forces us to find and connect to sources of light in our lives. If we let it, pain can become an impetus for building positive relationships that are mutually beneficial. When we process our pain, we stop looking for relationships to validate us and instead look for those that are balanced and that offer the support we need while allowing us to give of our best selves in a safe space where we feel valued and appreciated.

Pain teaches us to be more empathetic and humbler.
Processing the pain and my role in it allowed me to really see myself but it also allowed me to develop compassion for others who were dealing with their own distress and hurt. It also helped me to understand that the things we go through that causes pain in a way help to keep us mentally grounded and humble. Those living with pain recognize when others are living through it. Because of that we understand we are not alone and that no matter how "privileged" we feel we are, there is no one exempt from facing fears, suffering pain, being exposed to emotional abuse, or fighting to overcome life trauma. Pain doesn't care about your financial status, your physical appearance, your upbringing, or your intelligence. It keeps us from developing an attitude that believes we are above "going through" what others have

experienced. We realize that pain and trauma levels the playing field for all of us and we are fighting the war to live healthier mentally, physically, emotionally, and spiritually together.

When you experience emotional trauma and suffering it oftentimes means you have a heightened sense of other people's pain and suffering. I am truly at my core very soft-hearted and I am always saddened by other people's suffering. It is because of my own pain that I recognize I could be them, can remember times when I wasn't that far from being them, and know how quickly that misfortune can fall on anyone. One way that I feel led to help is by sharing my own personal life experiences. In doing so I hope my willingness to share will allow me to serve as a source of understanding and inspiration to those who are coping with their own pain. Without experiencing my own pain, I would not be able to even now be sharing this journey with you in the hopes that it could also help lead you to your place of healing. Processing my pain meant I had to become more vulnerable than I had ever been before and that wall I spoke about in earlier chapters began to crumble and come down.

By working through all these steps, our pain can become a source of strength instead of a hindrance. This process WILL take a while and become a continued work as it has for me, but the work will be worth it. I began to feel the shell of bitterness start to break away when I allowed God to reveal my shortcomings to me, as ugly and nasty and stinky as they were. This was the only way I could move forward on the path toward the BIG life I truly wanted to live.

Breaking up the root of bitterness you see is "me" work. It

requires you to take your focus off "what" and "who" happened and "why" and focus solely on "you". How were you impacted? How did you respond? How did you manage your response? How is that response still impacting your life today? God helped me understand my pain was valid, my hurt was real, and it did not go unnoticed by Him. My handling of it however was questionable. God had to shatter the shell of bitterness in my life before I could begin to shift toward living a BIG life filled with joy, peace, purpose, and destiny.

While revealing my own role was the first step toward healing, forgiving the other actors in the movie for the part they played was next. Let me take a moment to say that recognizing the unpleasantness of your role in your pain in no way absolves or diminishes the hurtful actions of others. Your pain and trauma could not be your fault however making peace with yourself and understanding how to protect yourself from it is your responsibility. There will be times in our lives when it is necessary to deal with those who hurt you head on in a constructive healthy way and this is vital to living a bold, inspired, and gifted life.

> **"**
> Breaking up the root of bitterness you see is "me" work. It requires you to take your focus off "what" and "who" happened and "why" and focus solely on "you".
> **"**

Knowing how to navigate conflict in personal relationships is essential to living healthy and free. However, for purposes of this process, I really wanted to focus on the internal work that we need to do to be our best. Dealing with the external is sometimes so much easier to do, it certainly was for me. I would much rather have lashed out or spent my time being angry at those who hurt me than taking a hard look at the things inside me that needed to be worked on.

This inner work that has to be done is the only way we can work toward building a life where we aren't paralyzed by fear. It is in this space where we do what is needed to realize our dreams and fully walk into our purpose and destiny. Forgiveness was necessary to bring the peace of mind and total healing to my life that I needed to do this. It will be critical to yours as well. Forgiveness is another thing in this process that isn't about anyone else but you.

To walk in true restoration and shift into this principle of living BIG, you must let go of the grievance, resentment, and anger toward those you feel have wronged you. Not doing so will cripple you and keep you from moving forward into your God-given potential. You must shift from walking in offense to running toward letting go and living free. Forgiveness does not mean forget; it just means you're able to move on. Forgiveness releases you from anger, thoughts of revenge, and feeling like you will be a stepping-stone to those who hurt you. I was stuck trying to keep myself from being hurt and walking in unforgiveness even though I had convinced myself I was "over it".

When I realized I had to forgive to move forward, it was hard. I began to list out to God all the things I thought had been done to me and by whom. God simply asked me, "How many times have I had to forgive you?"

Once I began to think on the many times, I have disappointed, hurt, and disobeyed Him, and the overall mess I was just because of my humanity and negative behaviors, forgiving became a whole lot easier. I ask myself this question every time I know I must forgive and find it hard to do so and every time it makes forgiving possible. The Bible reminds us of God's forgiveness and God's requirement that we also be willing to forgive.

> **❝**
> You must shift from walking in offense to running toward letting go and living free. Forgiveness does not mean forget; it just means you're able to move on. **❞**

"Bear with each other and forgive one another if any of you has a grievance against someone. Forgive as the Lord forgave you. And over all these virtues put on love, which binds them all together in perfect unity."
- Colossians 3:13-14,

Forgiveness opens the door to our healing and this healing can come in many ways, it may be instantaneous, or it could take some time. No matter what, please know that if you stand on God's word and remain in constant fellowship with Him, your feelings will line up with the Word of God and you will be able to be healed and find peace.

Being able to process pain by acknowledging it, praying about it, healing through it, and learning from it has been the reason I have been able to use my shortcomings or weaknesses to fully tap into my strengths. It is so vitally important that you allow God to reveal and heal the areas in your life that need the most work. Once you allow yourself to begin this process, you can begin to shift from living life in survival mode to thriving in a BIG way.

Prayer #3: God, I thank you that no matter where I am in life, I can trust you to always be there. You will never leave me or forsake me and for that I am truly grateful. I pray Father that you would allow me to remember to cling to your presence in my life as I continue to do the work to overcome fear to fulfill your purpose in my life. Please reveal those areas in my life where I am strong and shine your light on those areas where I am weak. Equip my heart to accept the things about me that I have been unwilling to see and please Lord guide me into the steps needed to change them so they will not impede my destiny. God help me to walk in forgiveness each and every day. I ask that you forgive me and forgive those who have hurt me in any way. Each and everyday Father, heal those wounds inside me and allow me to use my pain as a catalyst for progression. Help me to not only recognize your voice but to obey it. In your name I pray, Amen.

Big Step #3: Using the piece of paper you worked with in Chapter Two, complete the bottom two quadrants: How Can I Maximize My Strengths? and What Areas Do I Need to Improve?

Journal Entry #3: Make two lists: (1) The name of people you feel led by God to forgive and (2) The hurtful and painful things you need God to heal and deliver you through and from. Resolve to pray over these lists daily and allow God to lead and guide you through the forgiveness and healing process.

Chapter Four

BIG Moves: Getting past fear to welcome opportunities and blessings
RELEASING THE PAST, WALKING INTO YOUR FUTURE!

One of the skills I am most gifted in is being able to plan and organize big picture things into small workable steps and processes. I have been blessed with an uncanny ability to be able to take broad level visions, plans, and ideas and map out from start to finish how they can be realized. I absolutely love strategically planning something and then watching it unfold and become this great thing that it was visualized to be. Here is the irony about this great gift of mine, I have used it to successfully help at work, at church, to help family and friends, and even strangers at times. However, every time I have attempted to apply it to my own life, it has become nothing more than a stagnant blueprint. I've taken the plan and set it aside and forgotten about it or if I'm being completely honest (which I promised you I would be), I've ignored it because I was too afraid of failure to even begin to try and start to work the plan. Remember how I started off this book talking about how many of my dreams were unrealized and unfulfilled. This is the main reason why! You see, no matter how great the plans were, I never fully believed I was good enough to achieve them. The greatest fear was that the world would never see beyond my size to allow the beauty of my gifts and talents to shine through. Past experiences led me to believe I would never be accepted enough to accept the fruits of my dreams and passions. I wasn't confident and had no belief in my gifts and talents. I was disconnected from the amazing blessing that was given to me by God and the fundamental truth that not only was I created by God, but I was also equipped and prepared for it by Him also.

To "get over myself" so to speak and begin to adjust my behavior to reflect the greatness of God in me, I also had to once again recognize the very hurtful truth that I didn't have a world problem. I had a "me" problem. It wasn't how the "world" saw me that kept me from achieving, it was how I saw myself. I lacked the self-confidence to shake off the fear that paralyzed me because I had convinced myself that I would never be good enough, popular enough, smart enough, pretty enough, or thin enough for people to care anything about my gifts, dreams, and goals. God continually reminded of a key thing that I want to share with you in the hopes that you will read it, embrace it, rest in it, and act on it: You have been created for the very thing you're too afraid to do! That purpose and desire you have, to do the thing you've been procrastinating to start, it is not there by accident or happenstance. It has been birthed in you by the one who breathed life into your very existence. You have been chosen and called!

Another amazing thing about God is that no matter what, He will never reject you! He is the who called you and He is the one who will take care of you. He will be there with you through the fear, the uncertainty, the doubt, the guilt, the mistakes, and the failures. He will rejoice with you and for you throughout your entire process of Living BIG and becoming everything you have been predestined to be. Fear can either paralyze you or mobilize you, but we get to choose how we allow it to impact us. In the words of Soledad O'Brien, renowned journalist," I've learned that fear limits you and your vision. It serves as blinders to what may be just a few steps down the road for you. The journey is valuable, but believing in your talents, your abilities, and your self-worth can empower you to walk down an even brighter path. Transforming fear into freedom - how great is that?" Change the lens of your looking glass! See yourself better!

> **" You have been created for the very thing you're too afraid to do! "**

Another foundational truth for you to build your courage upon is understanding that when God created you, He placed everything inside you that you would need to fulfill your destiny. The God we serve is detailed and accurate. He is a precise God who pays attention to even the most miniscule details when He is planning the life, He wants us to live and have. He has intricately knitted together every facet of what you would need and what it would take for you to live BIG and achieve all your dreams.

> **" When God created you, He placed everything inside you that you would need to fulfill your destiny. The God we serve is detailed and accurate. "**

He gave you the circumstances, the strengths, the ingenuity, the gifts and talents, the character, and yes, even the right trials and tribulations to be 100% capable and equipped to walk out and thrive in your predestined purpose.

Nothing inside of you, not even your flaws, can prevent you from achieving greatness once you begin to tap into the reality of who

God is and who He created you to be. Know that God made you as an original version, you are valuable, worthy, and a rare treasure more precious than silver and gold. God created a masterpiece when He created me and when He created YOU. Start to see yourself accomplishing your dreams, being stronger than your trauma, healthier than your pain, and greater than your fear. One of my favorite scriptures can be found in Isaiah 41:10 (King James Version) where God tells the Israelites to:

"Fear not, for I am with you;

Be not dismayed, for I am thy God.

I will strengthen thee;

yea, I will help thee;

yea I will uphold you with the right hand of my righteousness"

As many times as I had read it, heard it and repeated it, I had forgotten it as a fundamental and necessary precept to realizing my dreams and overcoming fear paralysis. Fear paralysis is a very real thing! How many of you have attempted to begin something new or try something you're afraid to do, and you get a sick feeling in the pit of your stomach? Your mouth and throat go dry, you heart starts pounding, and you can't catch your breath. All these things are ways in which fear physically manifests itself in our lives. Fear literally can cause our brains to stop functioning, it undercuts our happiness and if we allow it to, it will hold us back from everything we desire to achieve in our lives. I bet that like me, you too can look back over your life and my unrealized dreams and clearly identify times when you allowed fear to keep you from taking a chance on achieving a dream or taking a leap of faith into the unknown.

However, I can tell you that those times when I learned how to embrace the fear and allow it to push me past my own personal hang-ups have been the most rewarding experiences of my life. For example, owning my own business has been a dream of mine since I was little girl who grew up watching and admiring her grandfather provide for and support a family of 11 with an elementary school education by owning a community grocery store, farming, and gardening. He was the hardest working man I've ever known but I can't remember a time when I saw him grumpy, or frowning, or seeming unhappy. To me, he always exuded peace, joy, and love. I knew I wanted to find that same thing some day by having my own business as well.

Before I took the leap into entrepreneurship, I spent many of my working years being able to sow into the lives of college students on college campuses in positions that were truly fulfilling. I met some of the most amazing people and spent time in a myriad of roles. But if I'm being honest, I didn't always feel like I was doing the thing I was destined to do with my life. My passion rested with being able to sow my gifts and talents into building a business that was my own. However, every time I attempted to pursue the dream of entrepreneurship, I allowed Imposter Syndrome to stifle my potential and keep me chained to the work force.

Imposter Syndrome is the belief that you are not as capable and competent as other people may see you. In other words, you feel as if you are a phony and that you don't belong in the spaces you've created or had created for you. For me, it meant not believing that I was skilled enough, gifted enough, liked enough, or supported enough to successfully build and launch a business. Work for me was "safe", I grew attached to the sure thing of having a steady paycheck. As a single young woman in her twenties raising my niece and nephew, it was also necessary. It was important for me to provide a stable home environment where they could grow and mature, and although we of course went through the same ups and downs of other families, I believed being committed to the stability a full-time job afforded us was more important than chasing my dreams. I did, however, use this time to earn my undergraduate and graduate degrees as well as work on my PhD. I was also able to spend time learning and gaining as much hands on experience as I could. I met many people who would become mentors and guides who allowed me the freedom to enhance my skills and nurtured my gifts. Their belief in me and push toward always developing professionally have served me tremendously on my entrepreneurship journey. I can now look back and see the value of my accomplishments and these relationships in a way that I could not before.

In April of 2021, I finally gained the courage through prayer to step out on faith and pursue my business full-time. I wish I could tell you this was an easy decision but of course it was not. I was terrified of losing the safety net of a sure thing, yet the courage to do it anyway, came from living out the very principles I have been sharing with you thus far in this book. It meant releasing the weight of oppression, trauma, affliction, and pain that I allowed myself to be under for years and beginning to adopt the identity given to me by God my Father. And each day brings its own share of challenges and rewards. Running a business full-time is not for the faint of heart. But I wake up every morning so excited and so free wondering what took me so long to finally say yes to my dreams.

It is essential to your journey that you also take the first steps to get outside of your own hang-ups whatever they may be and take the leap you need to begin changing your life for the better. Here is the crazy thing about fear, God didn't give you that, we are born virtually fearless. Fear is taught and can therefore be unlearned. Some key things you can do to help you shift beyond fear include:

- ACCEPT IT

Accepting fear as a reason you have not taken the first step in realizing your dreams is one of the most important steps to conquering it. Not only does fear sometimes keep us from starting, but it also keeps us from completing things and at times is even the reason why we self-sabotage and destroy things when we do build them. Fear is simply a feeling that can just like other emotions we experience come and go and either drive us or cripple us. When we choose to accept the fear, we take back our power over it. We can embrace it and in doing so use it to build our abilities to trust ourselves to conquer it. When we increase our trust in God and ourselves, we can then work toward understanding and embracing fear for our good.

- UNDERSTAND IT

You are not alone, everyone has experienced fear in some way, shape, form, or fashion during their life. Fear however provides us with an amazing opportunity to grow. At its very core though, fear can serve a great purpose in our lives; it is a natural human survival instinct. Would you know to run away from a wild tiger if you weren't fearful of it? Fear keeps us alive!

We must take the time to identify what we are fearful of and why. Once we understand this, it becomes possible to shift beyond how much of a threat our fear is perceived to be into how much of a threat it really is.

It is when our fear is allowed to become an irrational handicap that we must alter our behaviors and thinking. If you spend time really considering the things that fear you most, you will begin to see fear highlighting

> **"**
> When we increase our trust in God and ourselves, we can then work toward understanding and embracing fear for our good.
> **"**

the distance between where you are right now and where you want to be in the future. Fear will show you the very things that are holding you back from living your best life. In most cases, they are the things you're too afraid to think about, speak on, or unveil in the mirror. Begin to use your fear to recognize positive options in your life and tap into them as a booster cable to act. Be cautious but be bold!

- EMBRACE IT

It is impossible to get rid of fear completely from your life. As long as you are breathing and living, you will most certainly deal with some form of fear. You will never really stop being afraid, life just doesn't work that way. There will always be a curveball of some type that causes us to fear. Think about the recent pandemic that we are all living through.

No matter how fearless people claim they are, I am quite sure this recent global catastrophe caused a bit of fear in their hearts and minds at some point over the last two years. Embracing fear and not allowing it to paralyze you requires a mindset shift!

> **"**
> Begin to use your fear to recognize positive options in your life and tap into them as a booster cable to act.
> **"**

Embrace your fears by understanding how to use them to your advantage. Identify a reason why facing your fears head on and embracing them matter to you. For me, facing my fears meant becoming a better version of myself. It meant allowing myself to be more vulnerable, more open, and as a result to stop hiding myself from the world. Facing the fear of chasing my dreams makes me feel empowered and stronger than I've ever felt before.

The key thing is to start, not wait until you feel as if you have the optimal personal conditions to face, understand, and embrace your fear. Begin today, identifying your fears so you can move to embrace them and use them to help you grow. Learn how to master your responses to the fears so you control them, and they don't control you. When we start to embrace fear and use it for our own benefit, we can start to understand that we are more than capable of breaking through what has paralyzed us to propel ourselves into the action needed to reach our God-given purpose and Live BIG.

> 66
>
> Begin today, identifying your fears so you can move to embrace them and use them to help you grow. Learn how to master your responses to the fears so you control them, and they don't control you.
>
> 99

Overcoming or re-shifting the focus of your fears will allow you to move beyond the past and really walk toward your future. The most important word in that sentence is "walk". Notice that it is an action word that requires you to DO something. I have peppered this book with many action words in the hopes that you will be inspired to, WALK, LEAP, JUMP, GO, and yes, DO! I hope that you are now at the place where you are ready to complete all these things and more. Remember, in the words of John Burroughs," Leap and the net will appear".

One word of caution though, make sure you have a solid grasp of your "why" and be sure your vision and God's vision for your life are the same before you jump. What is the vision for your life?

"Where there is no vision, the people perish: but he that keepeth the law, happy is he"
                                                        -Proverbs 29:18

If you have limited vision, you will have limited success. Being able to identify and understand this vision will require time spent in prayer and reflection as well as the faith to act when needed. God is not some genie who is waiting for you to find a bottle, free him, and make three wishes. He is always near, and all we have to do is ask for wisdom and direction. James 1:5, tells us that, "If any of you lacks wisdom, let him ask of God, who giveth to all men liberally, and upbraideth now; and it shall be given him".

How awesome it is to know that God WANTS you to have a life filled with joy, passion, and purpose. When we ask Him to reveal our purpose to us, we can expect Him to give it to us. Once you pray for purpose, spend time in the Word of God to understand His heart and use His Word to bring light to places in our lives which seem darkest. Next be very clear about what your strengths and weaknesses are. What things do you do well? What things don't you enjoy? Being honest is key here as I am sure you know or have heard of many people who have spent years and years focused on things that had absolutely nothing to do with their purpose and have lived miserable lives as a result.

Being passionate about something can also be a pretty good determinant to what your purpose is. Do you like art, business, advocating for social causes, sports, etc.? God strategically uses both our passions and our gifts to help us identify our purpose. Above all else, be patient and trust God throughout the process. The process is just as much a part of walking in your purpose as finally fully operating in it is. When you are engaged in daily seeking God, doing the life work you need to becoming the best version of yourself, applying His principles, and sharing His love to impact the lives of those you encounter every day in a positive way, you are already operating in purpose.

Having a clear view of what you are working to accomplish and achieve, will be integral to your being able to overcome your fears. It is a journey that is well worth the effort it will take to complete it. Keeping your "why" in the front of your mind will help your focus as you work through your newfound strategy to accept, understand, embrace, and conquer your fears. Remember, being afraid is not uncommon, but you are also able to overcome this fear and use it as fuel to go after your dreams. It is totally possible that you will be able to turn the obstacle that was your fear into the opportunity you've been hoping for.

> **Prayer #4:** Father, please forgive me for allowing fear to consume and paralyze me. I recognize that you have not given me a spirit of fear but of power, love, and a sound mind. I reject any negative spirit of fear from operating in my life and I place my trust in you, knowing you are always

with me. Thank you for your help and your strength, thank you for protecting me and covering me. Please Lord give me the courage I need to be the person you created me to be. In your precious name, Amen.

Big Step #4: Vision Mapping

In order to become the person you were created to be, it is necessary for you to tap into the unique need God is leading you to become actively engaged in solving. This need is a shared responsibility, as you will become an intermediary God uses to share His solution with the world. God definitely does not need us; it is a privilege for Him to trust us enough to want to include us in doing His work and bringing glory to His name. Should He lead you to share his solution via speaking, writing, entrepreneurship, or some other means, it is vitally important to visualize the end goal.

Let's go back to the mirror you used in Big Step #1. Step in front of it, close your eyes and begin to visualize yourself doing one thing in your life that brings you the most joy. See yourself positively operating in it, allow yourself to feel the emotions connected to it, and embrace the power gained by accomplishing it. Open your eyes and "see" yourself in the here and now as the person you saw when your eyes were closed. That person IS you! Remember the vision of who you were when your eyes were closed and reference it whenever you begin to doubt yourself or feel inadequate. Use it as you work on the journal assignment below.

Journal Entry #4: A vision brings clarity, focus and alignment — synchronizing your time, efforts and energy towards what you really want.

This journaling exercise will help you do that.

Respond to the following statements:
1. (PURPOSE)I feel led by God to...
2. (PASSION)I am being directed by God to...
3. (PLAN OF ACTION) In order to do this, I must take the following steps...

Based on your responses to the questions above, what would you say is your life mission and God's vision for your life? Are they the same? Should they be?

Chapter Five

BIG REALITY: What voice are you hearing the loudest?
CELEBRATING YOU! SMALL STEPS REALLY MATTER

When you spend your entire life listening to voices and opinions that do not align with what the Creator has said about you, it becomes extremely difficult to accept that you are capable, strong, equipped, chosen, and destined to live a BIG life. Buying into everyone else's opinions and thoughts about who you are and what you can and cannot do can be quite dangerous and quite obstructive when it comes to walking in the blessings and opportunities God has for you. I am praying that as you read, you are beginning to learn how to squash the inconsequential voices that don't matter to you and that you are beginning to hear the voice of God more clearly. Listening to His voice is the only way you can move past the negative views you have adopted from others. In the words of renowned psychiatrist, C.G. Jung, "The world will ask you who you are, and if you don't know, the world will tell you."

In addition to moving beyond how others see you, it is also equally important to change the negative views of yourself that you have created and believed up to this point.

Learning who you came from, what the Creator says about you, and who He created you to be are critical to being able to celebrate instead of torment yourself because of your perceived shortcomings. It is so very easy to become a victim of self-criticism.

> " The world will ask you who you are, and if you don't know, the world will tell you.
> -C.G. Jung "

When you are constantly allowing negative thoughts about yourself to rest in your psyche, you automatically impose false limitations on yourself.

The more reasons you give yourself for why you can't do something, the more those reasons become valid to you and the more you believe your doubts. Simply put, when you believe you can't, you DON'T!

Let me pinpoint here that doing the work we spoke about earlier which allows you to identify areas of your life that need to be improved is not the same as allowing hurtful, negative internal views of yourself to grow and take up residence in your thoughts. There is a difference in recognizing the need to "be more productive" or "procrastinating less", than constantly telling yourself, "I'm such a big failure" or "I can't ever do anything right." Self-awareness is different from self-hatred and self-sabotage. One encourages a stronger sense of self-worth while the other can destroy your self-esteem and rob your peace of mind.

It is important that you commit to doing the work daily to overcome these negative thoughts and ideals that you've allowed to rule your thoughts and actions. Resolving to combat these thoughts that serve to destroy dreams is the only way to shift beyond your feelings of inadequacy. How YOU think about yourself is what matters. Making sure the way you see yourself lines up with how GOD sees you is essential. As an example, consider the muscles of the body. The ones you exercise the most function the best. When you fail to exercise and work out a specific muscle it begins to weaken and malfunction. Therefore, patients who have been bed-ridden for long periods of time are often prescribed physical therapy to rebuild their muscles and strengthen them so that they can function properly once again. This same principle can be applied to the way you think and feel about yourself.

You must commit to thinking and verbalizing positive affirmations and seeing yourself as a conqueror who is capable, powerful, and awesome EVERY DAY. Your thoughts reflect who you believe you really are, your thinking about yourself drives everything you do or in many cases don't do! Simply put, you are what you think you are! You must train your mind to be a muscle that uplifts, affirms, encourages, and even challenges you when you need it the most. If your inner thoughts about yourself are not strong, rehabilitate them! Everyday feed yourself with thoughts, affirmations, prayer, and insight into who God has designed you to be.

You are not your genetic background or economic status, you are not your job or position, or educational background. You are not your age, height, or weight. You are not your family's past or your own, you are not your mistakes, and you are not what you see as your failures. While these things may be how you are perceived or described, they are not who God says you are. God says you are unconditionally loved, capable, powerful, and wonderful. God says you have not been given a spirit of fear but of power, love, and a sound mind (II Timothy 1:7). God says you are strong, that you were created with purpose, that you are royalty, and that you are enough. Right here, right now, in this space, reading this book, in this moment and every moment that comes after it, you are enough!

Retrain your mind to embrace the truth about your character and not the lies you have been fed from others about who you are or the lies you've allowed yourself to construct that keep you stagnant, fearful, and emotional traumatized. We can only do this when

> **"**
> You must train your mind to be a muscle that uplifts, affirms, encourages, and even challenges you when you need it the most.
> **"**

we develop the practice of reconciling who God says we are with what we say, think, and feel about ourselves. I have learned to embrace and celebrate every bit of who I am, the good, the bad, and the ugly! Because all of it, every strength, every weakness, every flaw, was purposed and instilled in me by God. He knew what would be easy for me, what I would struggle with, what would challenge me, drive me, frighten me, attack me, and fuel me! Despite all of that however, I was still special enough to Him that He called me, predestined me, justified me, equipped me, and prepared me. Not only that, but every day, He loves me, provides for me, walks with me, guides me, leads me, and carries me when I am too weak to stand on my own. The most amazing thing about God is that He does this for ALL of us! We are all the same in His eyes. There is no person greater than you, better than you, or more capable of being you, than YOU!

It is imperative that you cut off the channels in your own brain and the toxic outside influences that have crippled and paralyzed you from being your best self and living your God ordained BIG life! Stop watching it, absorbing it, and recording it to play over and over again. CHANGE YOUR CHANNEL!! Begin to celebrate every bit of who you are and what makes you uniquely you. I empower you to be compassionate with yourself, put yourself first, take care of yourself, and move beyond the past messages that caused you to feel unworthy, incapable, and fearful. It is so much easier for us to be compassionate with others, however it is necessary that we also be kind to ourselves. Many studies show that there is a connection between how we treat ourselves and our mental health.

Being compassionate toward ourselves can reduce stress, anxiety, and lead to an increased overall sense of self-worth. Instead of criticizing or judging yourself harshly, give yourself permission to fail forward, learn from your mistakes, work on your shortcomings, and forgive yourself when you make mistakes or stumble.

Learning to love yourself will begin to allow you to strengthen your emotional toughness and heal from past hurts and trauma. Without self-care and doing the work to stay healthy mentally, physically, and emotionally, you are unable to fully function. Giving the best of yourself requires you to do what it takes to be your best. This was a very hard lesson for me to learn.

> **"** Be compassionate with yourself, put yourself first, take care of yourself, and move beyond the past messages that caused you to feel unworthy, incapable, and fearful. **"**

I spent many years of my life refusing to work on being healthy because I had convinced myself it was just another THING for me to do. It overwhelmed me, it required too much mental and physical action, and I just simply put my own needs behind the needs of my family, my job, my church, etc. What I know now that I didn't realize in my past was that I had to take care of me in order that I can be a more effective support to those around me. Getting to this place required me to deal with personal guilt about learning how to say no and being okay with choosing me first at times no matter how much other people pressured me to do things their way or to put them first.

I have cried far too many tears when the people I loved made me feel bad because I chose to challenge their treatment of me especially when it meant putting their needs before my own. I also spent a lot of time resenting them for doing the same thing for themselves I was trying to do. I realized that the people who I felt guilty about not helping had no problem not helping me when I needed them. It was easy for them to choose themselves first even when it meant my needs had to be sacrificed for them to do so.

As I write this, I chuckle a little to myself because you know what God's response to this was when I was praying and complaining to him about it? He simply told me to "Release the people in my life from my expectations of them". Can you imagine how shocking that was for me? God had once again shifted my focus from what was being done to me so that I could instead focus on what was really important which was my healing, my purpose, and my ability to allow Him to help me live BIG? See you can't live BIG when you would rather live stuck and spend your time focused on what was done to you, by whom it was done, and why they did it.

God challenged me to essentially, turn it over to Him and move beyond it. This was not easy for me to do. I had been wearing my hurt and pain like a cloak of honor for so long, I didn't even know how to remove it and I was so afraid of how exposed I would be when I undressed from it. Trust me this new you will be quite difficult to adjust to and embrace. It will require patience, understanding, and a whole lot of forgiveness on your part. But stay committed to your healing, your deliverance, your journey toward wholeness even when those you expect to love and support you, don't.

I would like to share with you the practical steps you can take to help develop this habit of self-love and self-compassion.

These are some things that have helped me on my own journey:

> You can't live BIG when you would rather live stuck and spend your time focused on what was done to you, by whom it was done, and why they did it.

Step #1 – Own your stuff

I talked a little bit about having to take an honest look at the person I was and the role I played in my own failures in an earlier chapter. The one thing you must realize even as you begin to celebrate yourself is that you are celebrating every part of who you are. It is okay if you have blemishes, imperfections, and weaknesses, we all do! It is okay to acknowledge the areas where you need work right along with praising the areas where you excel. Accepting the areas where you need to improve is not for the faint of heart. It was difficult for me to learn how to accept criticism that came from a place of love and support because so often in my life it came from a place of hatefulness and spite. But guess what, I have even had to learn to accept it when it comes from a place of hate as well. There is a huge sense of joy and accomplishment that you feel when you recognize that you have matured enough to be able to find the good even in things that were meant to cause you harm. However, whether coming from a place of support or harm, it can be used as a point of improvement and serve as a catalyst to inspire you to do the work needed to grow and develop into the wonderful being you have been called and destined to be.

There have been times when I have struggled with accepting and growing from my shortcomings. For example, my family and those closest to me have sometimes used the word stubborn as one of the ways they describe me. Whenever I heard it, it would automatically sound a negativity alarm in my brain. I would react to that alarm by being defensive and negative and blocking out anything that came after being described that way. However, through this process, I have had to really consider the ways in which my behavior has led those around me to see me as stubborn. I realized that I can be unyielding in my thoughts and opinions and not able to be swayed when I believe in something or believe a certain way about something. I can be very head strong and when I feel I am right about something, I rarely let anyone sway my thoughts about it. This was a hard pill to swallow because of course, I considered myself a very flexible and accommodating kind of girl. Being this way was after all my strategy for endearing myself to people despite my weight. Being flexible and likeable meant I was accepted and not rejected. At least that was what I had convinced myself of.

The more I considered it and prayed about it however, the more God revealed areas in my life where I had behaved as someone who was immovable and inflexible. This was one of many key areas I needed God to work on me to help me to get better. I could have very easily allowed this realization to derail the entire process of becoming the woman of God He intended me to be and let it spiral me back into the dark hole of self-doubt and depression I had so often lived in before. Instead, I asked God to show me when I was being stubborn and obstinate with others and help me to be more accepting and more accommodating. I can honestly say I see the progress in my thinking and actions because of this.

Two critical things I learned through this process: 1) Being stubborn is not always bad, it can also mean when I need to be, I am tenacious, persevering, and determined! I simply had to tap into the positive attributes and let go of the more negative ones, and 2) I will always have to consciously work on being more accommodating and flexible. No matter how much work I have done, the work must always continue. So, there are days when I applaud my efforts and there are days when I must honestly and truthfully tell myself that I need to do better. Either way, I must keep moving and I must own every fiber of who I am and who God made me to be. I must own it and not let my shortcomings own me.

Step #2 – Stop Seeking Outside Validation and Trust Yourself

When you seek validation, you are basically looking for another person's approval or looking for them to agree with your own sense of who you are. The issue however for many of us is that for too long we haven't had a true sense of our own self-worth and so we have allowed other people to build the perception of who we are and what our true value is. Desiring to have someone to agree with you is not a bad thing, at times it can be quite comforting to have a confidant, coach, or mentor that you are able to bounce ideas off and who can validate your thoughts or feelings about certain life happenings or life goals etc.

This becomes an issue however when we begin to allow other people's opinions and their agreement to shape our own decisions and to change the course of our life in negative ways that don't line up with God's purpose and plans for us.

> **"**
> There is a major difference between asking for advice and being completely dependent on it to make life altering decisions.
> **"**

In other words, when your voice or the voice of God is no longer the loudest voice you hear, there is a problem! There is a major difference between asking for advice and being completely dependent on it to make life altering decisions. Doing this becomes a detriment to our own well-being and we began to lose the power to allow God to guide our lives and to make strategic decisions based on His influence.

Some of the words used in the Merriam-Webster dictionary to help define the word validate are make legal, grant official sanction to, confirm the validity of, to support or corroborate, to recognize, establish, or illustrate the worthiness of. When considering these words, it is easy to ascertain that to validate something you must have some modicum of perceived power over the person or thing you are validating. You believe that you have the knowledge, the right, and the authority to determine the value of something. This perceived power can be such a destructive thing if placed in the hands of the wrong people for the wrong purpose.

There is no one person, not one, who should have the power to validate you, except the one who created you, God alone! Consider this, if you purchase an item and it arrives and does not work the way you expected, who do you contact? In most cases, you would contact the maker of the item to get a resolution and figure out how to make it work. If you own an Apple product for example, you most likely would never call Samsung to figure out how to repair it and vice versa. So then when it comes to your own self-worth, self-views, and self-importance, why are you consulting with anyone other than God your Creator?

The danger in constantly seeking the validation of other people is that when their ideas and opinions don't line up with what we see and think about who we are, it can oftentimes lead to depression and anxiety. We grow increasingly more agitated and unpleased with ourselves when trying to work toward being who "the world" says we should be in the hopes that they will like us, accept us, support us, and "validate" us. The more we allow this to happen the more we lose our own ability to look inside and see our own strength and power and be okay with who God says we are and who we believe ourselves to be. I am a living testament to the power of praying and seeking God to affirm who I am in Him by virtue of being His child, His creation, and His heir.

Unfortunately, though, I am also an example of what happens when you allow other people's opinions to establish your own sense of who you are and how you perceive yourself. I can remember being tormented constantly by those around me about my size from a very early age all the way through high school. I was constantly ridiculed, even by those who thought they were helping by bringing my weight to my attention over and over, giving me unsolicited advice about how I could be smaller. Emotionally and mentally all these things just made me do the exact opposite of what their advice was.

In school, some peers and even adults were super cruel. I spent much of my time in school nursing emotional scars. I felt inadequate, unpopular, and ugly. Of course, I was a master however at disguising my pain and so I was "busy" joining clubs and running for offices and participating in "things" once again in the hopes that my "works" would allow those around me to look beyond what I saw and felt they saw as my shortcomings. Yes, I was the fat girl, but I didn't let that stop me from doing great things, at least that's what I wanted everyone to think and believe about me. As I discussed in Chapter Three; I became a master at hiding my pain. I was determined to prove everyone who caused me pain wrong but in essence I was a mess inside.

I spent way too many hours analyzing how my peers and other people felt about me and how they saw me. What I should have been doing is figuring out why I allowed external opinions and behaviors to dictate how I saw myself. But alas, I was a child and not one who was strong and bold enough to be in the frame of mind to delve that deeply into my inner emotions. At the very core, I just wanted my peers to like me, to treat me better, and to be included. I wanted those members of my family who weren't supportive and loving to love me and accept me no matter what, but in their own way, some of their efforts to try and help me led to their hurting me even more.

My truth was that I heard negative words like fat, pig, elephant, hippo, tubby, whale, most of my childhood life and even at times in my adult life also. I've been told fat people smell bad and questioned about my hygiene just because of my weight. I heard, "You are so pretty, you just need to lose some weight" so much that I believed my size meant I was unattractive and ugly. I've been made to feel as if my very presence was a bother and annoyance by people I thought were my friends and so sad when I found out about events and activities to which I had not been invited.

I distinctly remember being told very clearly by my own father one day, when I announced as a child I wanted to grow up and have a family, that "No man is going to want to be with someone as big as you are." Unfortunately, my father was the source of some deep emotional wounds when I was growing up. I truly desired to be able to find safety in His presence, to find love, acceptance, and peace but instead I found fear, ridicule, and pain. In the only way he knew how, in many ways my own Father thought that by insulting me, provoking me, pointing out my faults due to my weight would inspire me and motivate me to do something about my weight and be healthier. It didn't, the words he used which just crushed me and wounded me.

But I do believe that in the only way he knew how, he wanted to push me so that life would be better for me. Unfortunately, his methods were not the best and I am in no way excusing how inappropriate they were. I needed my earthly Dad to be everything I have now found my Heavenly Dad to be but he was also only human. He had his own emotional battles to fight, his own fears to overcome, his own battle scars to heal from. Thankfully, my Father and I through some forgiveness, heart work and growing in our relationships with God, were able to heal our relationship. In the years leading up to his death in 2014, I felt accepted, loved, supported, and knew that he was proud of me when he departed this earth.

I am mature enough now to also understand that in many cases, some people truly do not understand the power of their words or the impact of their actions. This in no way condones their behaviors or absolves them from learning how to be kinder and think beyond themselves to see how their words and actions impact others, but it helped me to understand some of why it happened. Even in their attempts to help or "shock" me into changing, their behaviors only served to make me feel worse. The greater travesty is that their comments and treatment greatly influenced the way I saw myself and shaped who I became. I believed I was fat, unpretty, lazy, and unlovable for a very long time.

I wish I would have been strong enough to take away the

power of their influence over my life and my views about myself. I wish I had known then what I know now, and I wish my life had been filled with people who could have shared some of the powerful truths I am sharing in this book with me but it wasn't. That is another reason why I felt led and compelled to write this book. I truly hope that there is someone reading this right now who will be freed from the opinions and views of others and who can stand strong in their inner power and realize that when you "own" every bit of who you are, you take away the power for anyone else to define you!

It is possible, but to do so you must stop trusting them more than you trust God and more than you trust yourself. We must see ourselves, love ourselves, nurture ourselves, forgive ourselves, and yes even improve ourselves with grace and direction from God our Creator in order to walk in the power of self-validation so that we aren't looking outside of ourselves for the definition of who we are and who we should be.

It has become very simple for me and I hope it will be for you as well. Because God says I am beautifully and wonderfully made, I AM! I am an awesome, amazing, powerful, intelligent, gifted, and blessed woman of God! I walk in that truth daily and

> **"** When you "own" every bit of who you are, you take away the power for anyone else to define you! **"**

there is nothing anyone can tell me to change it. Even more importantly, I am not looking for anyone outside of myself to confirm it, to support it, to corroborate it, or to recognize it! Remember Chapter Two's Big Step? Who are you according to God? That is the only thing that matters. Do the work needed to align your view of yourself with the Creator's view and purpose for you. You truly are amazing, so start acting like YOU know it!

Step #3 – Shield your gifts and protect your peace

When God began to help me understand my purpose and why I was created, and to line up my views of myself with what His vision of me was, I also had to learn how to quiet down all the voices in my life that continued to feed me opposing information. See, even when we get to a place where we can boldly stand in the power of our destiny, it doesn't mean the voices which we allowed to negatively shape us in the past, even our own, automatically stop speaking to us. There will ALWAYS be people and things around us that provide opportunities for us to shape the image of who we see when we look in the mirror.

Our responsibility must be determining who God said we should see and who we want to see when we take that look. Once we know this information, we must begin the process of continually filtering out those things that do not constructively line up with who we are. We must work very hard every day to rid ourselves of the views and opinions that are cruel, hurtful, cause emotional scarring, or say anything different from what our Creator tells us about who we are. We cannot allow them to get into our inner sanctum, our heart, our mind, our body, and our soul. We simply have to block them from infiltrating our thought processes and our lives. How do we do this?

By understanding that no matter where you are in life and what you do, there will always be someone consciously and subconsciously watching you and forming opinions about you. But your responsibility to yourself is to know and embrace the understanding that what you will not ever be able to do is control what they think or see or what their opinion is about you or anything you do. Most importantly, while you can't control their thoughts, opinions, or actions, you can most assuredly control how you respond to it!

Oftentimes, other people project their own opinions about themselves onto those around them. Therefore, it is critical for you to learn how to keep anything that is counterproductive, counterintuitive, and causes you to regress into a place where you feel inadequate, from having access to your inner thoughts, feelings, and emotions. You must adopt a "No Access Granted" frame of mind. You must find peace with who you are and love yourself! You must resolve to take full responsibility for your own happiness and not look to other people to provide it for you. To be completely free, you have to earnestly pray and ask to be delivered from other people's opinions about you. Frankly put, their opinion of you is their own problem!

Here's another thing though, I am not just talking about negative opinions, there is also danger in always seeking out and listening to only positive opinions. The goal is not just to surround yourself with people who agree with you, only tell you the nice things you want to hear and overlook when you've done something wrong or where you could need improvement. Doing this

> **"** Keep anything that is counterproductive, counterintuitive, and causes you to regress into a place where you feel inadequate, from having access to your inner thoughts, feelings, and emotions. **"**

means you leave yourself with no room for personal growth. Making room for personal growth is essential to be able to see not just where you are but where you can go.

Coupled with our personal relationship with God, it is what allows us to change our thinking and open our eyes to the real potential that resides inside of us. It is also what gives us the belief and courage we need to go after our dreams. The point of this book is not to lead you to a place where you believe there is no room for you to improve but rather to help you be more self-aware and tuned in to the true motives of those around you. "Surround yourself with people that push you to do better. No drama or negativity. Just higher goals and higher motivation. Good times and positive energy. No jealousy or hate. Simply bringing out the absolute best in each other." -Warren Buffet

You need family and friends who can give you constructive criticism which comes from a place of love and a sincere desire to see you win and be your Bold, Inspired, and Gifted self! You have to know the difference between constructive feedback and hurtful negative opinions from those that don't mean you any good. Feedback from loved ones should be given in such a way that you know their true intent is to help you improve and develop. This feedback can come with a soft wind when needed, but it can also come with a forceful gale as well. How it is delivered is oftentimes contingent upon your openness to receiving it.

There are times in my life when a soft kind word is enough and then there are others when I need a stronger more authoritative voice to help me "get it". Constructive criticism should be focused on helping you to improve your actions and behaviors not on demeaning or belittling you. For example, there is a marked difference between saying, "You spoke to someone in a rude manner which was not okay. I really need you to be careful that your words are kind and not disrespectful or hurting" versus, "You are rude, disrespectful, and nasty. That's why people don't want to be around you, you will never have any friends except me." Which one would you respond to and consider?

Words and opinions that make you feel demeaned, sad, attacked, tear you down, and that cause embarrassment should be ignored and rejected. Doing this effectively means practicing it more and more every day. It will be tough at first to change your behaviors and not to react by shutting down and internalizing every unkind word. But the more you purpose in your mind and heart to keep those types of comments, behaviors, attitudes, and people outside of your inner circle and innermost thoughts, it will become easier to do so. Learning how to shield my gifts and protect my peace, meant I first had to learn to give myself permission to be okay with NOT having certain people in my life and NOT being certain places, and NOT participating in certain activities. This wasn't easy, but it was absolutely necessary!

You will find yourself amazed at how peaceful and positive your life becomes when you are delivered from people and things that don't mean you any good and that don't bring you any joy, I know I did. Stop seeking out things that destroy you! Because the truth of the matter is, the reason why you're so focused on what others say and feel about you, is because you need them to fill up your bank of self-worth. You're looking for someone to fill that bank with love and positivity and in doing so give you a feeling of pride and accomplishment so you can make regular withdrawals and then have them make additional deposits as needed.

Well, here is a cold hard truth, that bank will never be full until you can fill it up yourself! Take ownership and responsibility for your own life. Forget what they think or said, forget about what they attempted to deposit in that bank, what did YOU think, what did YOU say about YOU, what did YOU deposit in that bank? This is the only thing that matters.

Your focus should be on connecting to the Creator as your source of light and inspiration. I cannot express enough (that's why I am expressing it again here) the importance of really spending time developing an understanding of what He says about you and using that to develop your own sense of inner truth and strength. Forget everything else and let the "light" that is your new self-awareness, self-worth, and self-esteem, be your only response to hate and negativity.

Your "glow up" will be so bright, they won't be able to focus on anything else! Stay committed to your goal of living a life that honors the greater purpose God has placed inside of you. When you take the time to do this, you will be so consumed by achieving your dreams and walking into your destiny, you won't have time to worry about what others say, think, or feel about you. Do not allow them to consume your time, instead spend your time redeeming the time you lost living beneath the privilege and grace God has afforded you.

Go out there and start living BIG, without apology, with interference, without barriers and watch God do amazing things through you and for you. You are the apple of God's eye; He loves you unconditionally and He believes in you! Not only that, but He

> **"**
> Stay committed to your goal of living a life that honors the greater purpose God has placed inside of you.
> **"**

also values you enough that He promised never to leave you or forsake you in the Word. There are some special people in my life who constantly remind me that I am a rare and treasured jewel, and the world has need of every great thing God has instilled inside of me! I want to share these same words of encouragement with you, because the amazing thing about God is that He doesn't just feel that way about me and He didn't just uniquely gift and call me, He did that for every single person He created and that means YOU are included!

Prayer #5: Heavenly Father, I thank you for every blessing in my life both great and small. I thank you for the gift of life that you bestow upon me every day. There are no words that can truly express how thankful I am to be your child and to know that I am constantly in your thoughts. I pray that you would please lead me and guide me as I venture through this journey toward self-fulfillment and seeing myself the way you see me. Please Lord, break every chain of bondage, every negative word of failure and unworthiness, and ever stronghold in my life that would cause me to operate outside of your plans and purpose for me. I ask that you free me from every negative word, deed, and action that has been said about me, been done to me or that is being planned for me. I stand firmly on your word that tells me that no weapon formed against me will prosper. I decree and declare that I am more than a conqueror through you and that I am victorious in every area of my life. I pray that you would give me the strength, courage, and boldness I need to separate myself from anything that is meant to harm me or hinder me, including my own thoughts and desires. I thank you Father for giving me everything I need to walk freely and boldly into the future. In your mighty name, I pray, Amen!

BIG Step #5: Let's go back to the mirror. Once again, step in front of it, close your eyes and count to ten. Open your eyes verbally speak aloud, six (6) positive things about yourself. Three (3) of them should be physical and three (3) non-physical. Now, think about the negative thoughts and opinions you have allowed to keep you stuck and oppressed? Remind yourself why you now know they aren't true.

Journal Entry #5: How can you use your current values and knowledge of who you are in God to shift negative thoughts into positives? Write down three tangible things you plan to do to retrain your brain and adopt a new vision of self beyond past negative images from others and from yourself?

Now think about some of the times in your life when you have been most proud of yourself. How did you feel when they were done? Did you allow yourself to be proud? Did you reward yourself? Did you celebrate? If you could go back and relive them, how would you change the way you reacted to your accomplishment?

Chapter Six

BIG SHIFT: Stop Apologizing and Start Living BIG
PURSUING YOUR PASSION, FINDING YOUR PURPOSE

I truly pray that one of your main takeaways from the last chapter is the revelation that your only responsibility to the world and to those around you are to live a life where you can be 100% authentic about who you are and what you have been placed on this earth to do. Becoming your authentic self however means first giving up on your efforts to "be" somebody else. I have learned in my honest assessment of myself, and I think this is true for many people, we have spent our entire lives trying to be anybody other than who we are. When you have felt demeaned, oppressed, unsure of yourself, and have listened to the voices of those around you who fed you negative opinions about who you were, it becomes very difficult to not only walk in your authenticity, but to even know who your authentic self is. We not only desire to be someone else, but we spend a lot of time comparing ourselves to others around us.

Measuring our own success, worth, and value based on the life of someone else can be quite a dangerous thing. We sometimes give so much attention to what other people do, we can't even explain, rationalize, evaluate, or express what's going on in our own lives. Do you know what happens when cars travel into someone else's lane? They crash! This is exactly what happens to us when we try to live our lives in the same way as those we admire, respect or even envy. Their lives become the measuring stick by which we gage our own success and failure. Please don't misunderstand me, it is perfectly okay to admire good qualities in someone, to appreciate someone's accomplishments, or to use their stories as a source of inspiration. It is a very different thing however when doing so means you are incapacitated by the sense of never measuring up to their example. When your admiration becomes the cause of personal pain and self-doubt then it is no longer healthy.

Constantly comparing yourself to others and convincing yourself that you don't measure up to whatever invisible plumb line you use to determine your self-worth, often leads to depression, low self-esteem, bitterness, and envy. In the words of Theodore Roosevelt, "Comparison is the thief of joy." You are running a race that you will never win. There will always be someone better at something than you are. And that's okay because their race is theirs and your race is uniquely yours.

The goal is not to be the best "at something" the goal is to be the best "YOU" possible. The very people you are comparing yourself to have their own internal struggles, personal issues, and challenges. I can assure you that you are not seeing the whole picture, you are only seeing what you've been allowed insight into. They are presenting you with the best version of themselves. But if given the opportunity to look closer, you will see they are fighting their own battles and demons. Remember the old cliché' the grass isn't always greener on the other side? Well the lens through which you evaluate someone else's life isn't always clearer. Give yourself grace and please let go of the drive toward perfectionism.

Freeing ourselves from the practice of comparing ourselves to those around us means we can have laser focus on meeting our own goals. It means we aren't spinning around every day like a hamster on a wheel chasing these elusive dreams that were never supposed to be ours in the first place. This is the reason why you're so exhausted and depressed. It's because you're running after a life that was never created for you and that was never ordained for you to have. God already gave you YOUR purpose, even if you don't recognize it yet! The wheel will stop spinning when you start pursuing THAT with the same fervor that you seek to be like those around you. If God wanted everyone to be exactly alike, He would have created us that way. You are an INDIVIDUAL, there is no other person exactly like you anywhere.

This is true even for identical twins, yes they may look exactly alike but their personalities are different and uniquely theirs. Your uniqueness is what makes you special, own it!

> **"**
> God already gave you YOUR purpose, even if you don't recognize it yet!
> **"**

There will never be another you to grace this world. Imagine how sad it would be to leave it knowing you spent all your time here trying to be someone else, trying to build their legacy instead of building your own. Focus on those things that are positive and learn to be grateful for God having embedded them into your DNA. Stop comparing and competing with others and focus on your own personal growth! Take the time to know your own strength and weaknesses, your own unique gifts and talents, your own purpose for being here.

This journey to knowing who you are and why you have been placed here will be at times unpredictable and challenging. It will lead you down a path where you must face your deepest fears, find the source of your self-doubt, expose your vulnerabilities, and acknowledge the things which make you insecure. This process requires you to spend time listening to what you feel is your deeper calling and the things that really matter in your heart. I pray that as you have worked through this book, it has helped you begin to really think about those qualities and attributes that God has uniquely given you. Why is this important? Because you have been placed here to fulfill a purpose and when that purpose is left unfulfilled, you are empty and unhappy, and always seeking joy in things that can never bring you true joy.

The gifts God has placed inside of you are there to serve a greater purpose and benefit society. You, yes YOU, matter! Your life matters, and everything you do in life impacts someone or something. If you have not begun to tap into those special qualities, it is okay because we will spend some time at the end of this chapter doing just that. All I ask is that you give yourself some grace and time to figure it out. There is no set time frame for how long this process takes, take as long as you need. Spend time intimately with God and allow Him to speak to you and reveal His will for your life to you. He will honor the commitment of your time and effort to complete the steps toward wholeness and embracing your divine purpose. There is no substitute for taking this time and walking through this process to develop a deeper, intimate fellowship with God. The wonderful thing about God is that He desires this relationship with us and makes it so easy to have.

Intimacy is achieved when we embrace the experience of knowing and being really known by another person. When we are intimate with someone, we "feel them", we are "connected" to them, we are "close" to them, we know them at a "deeper" level

> **"**
> Spend time intimately with God and allow Him to speak to you and reveal His will for your life to you.
> **"**

than others. The key component for developing intimacy is trust. In order to become intimate with God, you must first trust Him. In order to trust Him, you must first know Him. In order to know Him, you must simply spend time with Him.

Begin to speak to Him throughout your day in prayer and thanksgiving, spend time reading the Bible, and schedule time with Him so that He knows He is a priority in your life. I have come to value my time with God as the most joyful and most rewarding time of my days. In Him is where I find strength, direction, and peace. It is this strength, direction, and peace that I lean on in the best of times, worst of time, and in the in between times. It has been integral to my being in a space which allows for me to embrace who I am and who He has called me to be. It has allowed me to finally be free enough to live life BIG without apology.

I cannot encourage you enough to take the time to fellowship with God to allow Him to help you identify what your gifts and talents are and then lock into how He intends you to use them. When you tap into your gifts, talents, purpose, and passions:

- *Your life begins to take direction and as a result you can begin to feel good about yourself and about your future path.* It is not so much about knowing the "one thing" you are going to do but rather about having a greater sense of your self-worth and the peace that comes from knowing your life is in alignment with God's purpose for you. Embrace the journey and enjoy the process. The journey is a major part of your purpose. It is where you are molded and shaped. The journey is where the refining process happens. Understand that God's truth about you is the light you need to overcome the battle of self-doubt we fight against every day. The victory has already been won in this battle, it is ours because of who we are in Him and to Him. His truth is what we can be sure of, and His truth is the only thing that can help us be free from the chains of oppression, strongholds, and mental bondage we've lived with up to this point in our lives. As I have embraced these truths, I have been able to rest in who I am in Him and this freedom has meant I am secure in being me. I have a strength, joy, peace, and determination that I have never had before.

- *You understand the things you are good at, things you enjoy, and how you can use those things to contribute to the world.* Life becomes a lot easier because you focus your time and effort on the things that matter specifically to fulfilling your goals and purpose rather than focusing on things that don't positively impact you or those around you.

- *You gain a clearer sense of self-worth and increased confidence. You give yourself the grace you need to grow and cease being overly critical of yourself.*

This sense of self-awareness and ownership of your authentic self and unique purpose allows you to move forward on this journey toward Living BIG. Living BIG requires you to enter each day walking in a newfound sense of clarity and focus. It means operating fully in the very essence of everything that is YOU! It means living life without apology, and embracing all of who you are: strengths, weaknesses, thoughts, feelings, goals, dreams, fears, flaws, passions, desires, accomplishments, and failures. Living BIG is a direct result of allowing yourself to connect to your Creator and your purpose for being created. Living BIG means living outside the boundaries that have been imposed on you by others and living outside your own self-imposed restrictions about what you can and cannot do. For me, that has meant not being defined by my weight. It has meant focusing more on the size of my life and not the size of my body. For you it could mean something completely different, but it is critical for you to find the big "thing" that you must push past in order to have a BIG "life".

This notion of Living BIG was birthed out a desire to live life with purpose, intent, and without reservation. I reached a point in my life when I was "sick and tired of being sick and tired". I stopped blaming others for my misery, stopped seeking the answers to my problems from other people, and spent time maturing in my relationship with God. Gaining an understanding through prayer and connecting to God through reading His Word helped me realize that only He could fill the empty places in my life, places that I had tried to fill with so many other things that weren't equipped to provide it. It couldn't be found in food, men, friendships, materialistic things, personal accomplishments or work. I can assure you that I have at one point in my life, or another, tried to fill it with every single one of these. Until I allowed God total access to fill the empty places in my life with His love, His desires, and His purpose, I was unhealed, unfulfilled, unhappy, and empty.

Here is another truth moment, it is entirely possible to know God, love Him, say you're committed to your relationship with Him, and still NOT be connected to Him and walking fully in His love and grace. The reality is that I knew that God was a God of love, but I couldn't even begin to believe that He loved me. I was so caught up in trying to "prove" myself worthy of love and acceptance from everyone around me, I began doing the same thing to God. I didn't love myself so I couldn't possibly grasp His love for me. When I began to really open myself to allowing Him to minister to my heart, mind, body, and soul through His word, He began to help me see just how wrong I was.

The amazing thing about God's love is that it truly is unconditional and there is absolutely nothing we can do to change it or cause Him to take it away. There is nothing we can ever do to deserve it, but He doesn't ASK us to do anything but accept it. His love for us has nothing to do with us and everything to do with Him. His love is all powerful and that is why it is so critical for you to accept it and allow it to work in your life. His love is what we need to move beyond fear, heal from broken hearts and wounded souls, move past pain caused by rejection, and change the behaviors associated with self-doubt and self-sabotage that we have been operating in. Know that God loving you is not a mistake, His love for you didn't have to grow or be cultivated. He loved you from the moment He knitted and formed you before He deposited you into your mother's womb. God CHOSE you and He

CHOOSES to love you every day!

When you begin to believe the awesomeness of God's love for you it will allow you to truly know your value, find the acceptance you have been so desperately seeking, and push forward toward recognizing and fulfilling your purpose. Basking in His love and tapping into the power source of His word daily, you will find it is much easier to operate from a place of grace in your life and in how you deal with others, but you will also find it so much easier to embody the precepts of Living Big that are the cornerstone of this work: Boldness, Inspiration, and Giftedness!

There is so much power to gained from actually liking yourself. When you allow yourself to truly love who you are despite your flaws, hang-ups, and mess ups, you essentially open the door for growth. Knowing that God approves you should be everything you need to approve yourself. You can release the bonds of guilt, low self-esteem, self-destructive behavior, and inferiority you've allowed to permeate your life.

Recognizing and owning your identity in Him means His favor is allowed to operate freely in your life. He can then work on shaping and molding you into the person He created you to be.

> **"**
> God CHOSE you and He CHOOSES to love you every day!
> **"**

I knew that pushing beyond the image and thoughts about myself that I had allowed to grow from my own feelings of inadequacy and be birthed out of the opinions and poor treatment from those around me, would mean a complete and total transformation from the way I had been thinking and would require me to step outside my comfort zone to live life differently. Living Big is about giving yourself permission to dream and have a vision for your life. It is about believing you can do extraordinary things and color outside the lines of your own boundaries. It is about recognizing your gifts and focusing on putting them to use in the way God intended. Living Big is about understanding that with God, all things are possible! Let us break down the three tenets for doing so: Boldness, Inspiration, and Giftedness.

Living Bold

When you begin to understand and recognize the greater purpose for your being here on Earth, there will be a compelling sense to begin doing something to fulfill it. For me, this sense of urgency to do something however was also matched with an overwhelming feeling on inadequacy and fear that I would never be able to walk in my purpose the way God intended. Expressing this to God however provided Him the opportunity to as I stated earlier, remind me that I already had everything I needed to operate in my purpose. Not only that but it had ALWAYS been there, God was just waiting on me to activate it. Another truth that helped me move past my own sense of fear and inadequacy, the understanding that God would be walking WITH me and the Holy Spirit would be guiding me every step of the way. You will never be alone when you walk with and develop an intimate relationship with God. He is ever present with you and in the times when you can't depend on your own strength or when you can't see your own value, remember to plug back into what He says about who you are and that you belong to Him so as He promised in His word, He will never leave you.

Fully embracing and operating in your purpose will require you to "do something" and press forward into the unknown. Having the presence of mind and the will to push past fear and inadequacy will require boldness. It will have to be embraced and it will have to permeate your every thought,

> **❝**
> Having the presence of mind and the will to push past fear and inadequacy will require boldness.
> **❞**

action, word and deed. Purpose requires it! You cannot be timid about doing the thing God has called you to do. Boldness simply means having the courage to act, speak, and move despite fear, risk, or obstacles. Boldness will give you the power to start and continue the journey to pursue your purpose with confidence. When you face each day boldly without apology, you can not only envision a better future for yourself, but you are also able to begin to help others manifest a better future for themselves.

> **❝**
> Boldness allows us to rise each morning and say, "Look out world here I come".
> **❞**

Boldness means shifting beyond what was and forging forward into what can be. It means facing every day with clear goals and without trepidation. Boldness allows us to rise each morning and say, "Look out world here I come". Live bold enough to be confident and fearless enough to face life head on and conquer anything that comes your way. Tap into the power instilled in you by our Father and boldly create the life you desire and deserve, and then live it fully!

Living Inspired

Living Inspired is all about showing up and living life regardless of the outcome. There will be wins and losses, achievements and failures, but no matter what you must show up to even get in the game. We cannot let fear, self-doubt, or rejection keep us from boldly living a life filled with joy.

Once you have begun to live life outside the boundaries of your own fears and insecurities and those set upon you by others, it is important that you tap into ways to continue to stay motivated and committed to walking toward your purpose and fulfilling your destiny. Living an inspired life requires you to connect to those things that make you feel joyful and vibrant. Inspired living means you embody and outwardly portray the gifts, purpose, passion, and destiny placed inside of you by our Father. Living Inspired means, you realize that you understand your light does not just shine for you, but it lights the pathway for those around you as well. When we live inspired, we are more able to look beyond our limits and experiences and explore new possibilities. It can completely transform the way we think about ourselves and our capability to manifest our dreams.

It also means living fully in the moment enjoying every moment of life and every step of our life journeys no matter what obstacles, barriers, or circumstances we face. Living in the moment however was very hard for me to learn to do. I am a thinker by nature, a planner, and I tend to over analyze the simplest of things. Oftentimes this results in analysis paralysis, and I overthink so much I tend to do nothing at all. I can think myself out of almost anything. In doing so, I often forget to just stop and take a moment to enjoy life right where I am, in the present moment, in the right now!

On this quest toward Living Big however, I had to learn that it is critically important to be "present" for every moment of every day. It is imperative not to overlook the joy of our present by focusing so much of our time and energy on our future or our past.

> **"** Inspired living means you embody and outwardly portray the gifts, purpose, passion, and destiny placed inside of you by our Father. **"**

Another essential thing to understand about living inspired is knowing that true joy is not directly tied to accomplishments, goals, or things. It is quite eye opening when we think about how much of our joy has been linked to "things". We are conditioned form an early age to seek outside of ourselves to find comfort, peace, and contentment. The truth of the matter however is that everything we need to live inspired and live on purpose is already within us. The things we are blessed enough to acquire on our life journey are just icing on the cake so to speak. They are blessings we receive from God and they should further enhance our joy not become the source. God is our source and only He alone can provide true inner peace and joy.

Living Inspired means resting in the understanding that we do not need anything else to have true joy and bliss except what God has already given us. No matter the circumstance, the challenge, the obstacle or the mountain you see before you, activate your faith and believe God for it to be moved out of the way.
This faith and understanding that God truly will work all things out for your good (Romans 8:28) will allow you to experience joy through every situation and that joy is critical to your ability to activate your purpose and share your gifts with the world.

Living Gifted

In our world, the meaning of someone who is gifted has oftentimes been commonly associated with students and adults who have demonstrated above average achievement capacity in academics and even in other areas such as arts and leadership. In the spiritual sense, I would

> " Living Inspired means resting in the understanding that we do not need anything else to have true joy and bliss except what God has already given us. "

like to challenge the worldview of what it means to be gifted by sharing that the word gifted can be more aptly described as not what special things a person does but who a person is. Even greater it is not something that is developed or that can be learned, giftedness is embedded into the very DNA of your holistic self by the Creator who made you. There is nothing we do to earn our gifts, we simply receive them through His lovingkindness, grace, and mercy. These gifts exist solely for the purpose of bringing glory and honor to God and for the benefit of others. When we use them to bless those around us by fully embracing and operating in our purpose, the Kingdom of God benefits.

Your gifts have been uniquely gifted to you for a specific purpose, if you don't accept them and use them, they lie in waste, never affecting the change God intended when He placed them inside of you. Every one of your gifts was placed there as an intentional

> " There is nothing we do to earn our gifts, we simply receive them through His lovingkindness, grace, and mercy. These gifts exist solely for the purpose of bringing glory and honor to God and for the benefit of others. "

mechanism to bless those around you. Your gifts are the answer to someone's needs.

If I could tell you how truly liberating it was to understand that MY gifts were placed inside of me with purpose and that I had everything I needed to achieve everything I had ever dreamed or felt compelled to achieve. I wasted so much of my life worrying about, envying, and admiring the gifts of those I felt were thinner, smarter, nicer, prettier, more popular, and the list goes on and on. So much of my stress and self-doubt came from fretting over other people's purpose and not tapping into my own.

I had to learn that by failing to recognize and appreciate them, I was being a poor steward of His gifts and thereby denying those around me and even those I had yet to meet, their opportunity to be blessed and be touched in the way God intended them to be through me. I had failed my assignment! I was so busy seeking outside of the source of all joy and happiness for contentment and peace, that I missed the opportunity to gain rewards greater than I could ever imagine. It was only when I allowed Him to truly heal my hurt, my pain and unlock the potential that was lying dormant inside me, that I was able to clearly see why I was here and what God has assigned for me to do.

When you finally look beyond your limited perceptions of who you are and embrace ALL of whom God made you to be, it will become possible for you to fully own the power of your gifts. You will begin to live life differently, you will be able to connect to the power of your own voice, thoughts, and opinions. You will find courage to delve deeper into the psyche of who you are and why you're here. Your giftedness is what will ultimately allow you to look in the mirror and realize that you are fierce, you are not broken, you are powerful, you are enough! Enjoy your journey!

Prayer #6: Thank you God for the blessings you have given to me and for the trials and tribulations I have been able to overcome with your strength, grace, and mercy. I humbly ask and pray that you would help me in this journey to live bolder, more inspired, and to fully activate every gift that you have given to me. Please reveal more of yourself to me, help me to know you fully and to live in a way that honors you as my Father. Your word instructs us to seek you with our whole hearts and then we will find you, so now I commit God to seek after you with all my heart and soul. Please direct my paths and show me how to have a more intimate relationship with you. Fill me with your Holy Spirit so that He can guide me and teach me to hear your voice and recognize your will for my life. Help me to face each day without fear, to have a clean heart, and to bask fully in the joy that you have given to your children. Sharpen my vision, increase my faith, and grant me the power to embrace and complete the work that you have placed in my hands. In Jesus' Name, Amen.

BIG Step #6: Self Love Sanctuary: Take a few minutes to find ten sheets of paper or ten index cards. On each card, write down one positive fact about who you are. Begin each statement with the phrase, "I am...". Once completed, find a quiet place at a time when you can really focus without distractions or interruptions. If you'd like, play some relaxing music and light some candles. If you play music, look for something instrumental without words and vocals. Find the most comfortable position for yourself, whether it be sitting in a chair or on the floor. Take a few moments to close your eyes and just be. Breathe in and out deeply. Relax your muscles and become very still. Begin to focus on the rhythms of your body. Feel your heartbeat, hear your breath, feel the sensation in your fingers. Spend some time simply being in that moment. Once you feel yourself completely relax and focused on the essence of who you are, begin to read aloud all ten (10) of your affirmation statements. Read them as many times as you'd like! Read them until your spirit lines up and connects with the words. End this time by making a special vow to yourself. Focus on honoring yourself and this vow every day until you have your next Self-Love Sanctuary time. Before you leave your sanctuary, determine when and how often you will revisit this exercise. I strongly recommend at least once a week. Doing this exercise affirms our self-love which builds our hope, increases our joy, and fills us with a newfound appreciation for our potential.

Journal Entry #6: One of the key tools in embracing and living life BIG begins with gratitude. Being thankful for all the blessings you already have oftentimes clears out the fuzziness that has clouded our brans when we've focused so much on the "others" in our lives. Commit to keeping a gratitude journal for the next seven (7) days. Before going to sleep at night, write down a list of all the things you are grateful for from that day. Divide your list into the following categories: Blessings I Received, and Blessings I Provided. Pray over your list before going to bed each night and thank God for the blessings given and the times you were obedient and gave of yourself to someone else. This could take many forms, it could be time, knowledge, financial, etc.

Chapter Seven

BIG MOVES: Rescue Yourself from the Island
SADDLE UP YOUR "POWER POSSE"

A big portion of the content of this book has been devoted to the "self-work" that is needed for you to live life boldly, inspired, and gifted. Another significant part of that process however is understanding and realizing the importance of developing and cultivating positive and mutually beneficial relationships with other people.

No matter how strong and independent a person is, there is an innate desire placed in us by God that requires us to lean on, depend on, grow with, learn from, and seek out others. For us to be successful in our journey of self-improvement, the true irony is, we cannot improve ourselves without others. Yes, you can achieve many things by yourself, but you can achieve even greater things with others. Allowing others into your inner sanctum may prove frustrating and challenging but even in the worst of times, these relationships cause you to grow. These "inside" influencers will become members of what I like to call your "Power Posse".

Your "Power Posse" will consist of those around you who you know will help you excel in your strengths but will help you to grow from your weaknesses. These will be persons you trust to not only affirm you but disagree with you when needed. Be sure you include people in your Power Posse who are diverse, have different skill sets, and have different outlooks on life. You are not looking for clones of yourself, you are looking for those around you who are "insiders" that you

> "For us to be successful in our journey of self-improvement, the true irony is, we cannot improve ourselves without others."

trust to go with you as you journey forward to walking in your purpose and living your BIG life. Members of your Power Posse will encourage you to grow in ways you may not have imagined and step outside of your comfort zone all while respecting the authentic you, your own beliefs, and your boundaries.

This is especially important because often it is extremely hard to motivate ourselves to step outside our comfort zone and the encouragement of those around us could help us do it so much sooner. Your Power Posse will contribute to your growth, not impede it! From a very early age, it was less painful to find things I enjoyed doing alone rather than be around people and situations where I would be subjected to negative comments about my weight and to ignore the hurt of not being included or invited to group activities. As a result, I also became isolated and spent much of my younger years without any close friends. For me, isolation became a defense mechanism. I separated myself from the people, situations, and memories that caused me to feel pain and emotionally instability.

I often tell people that I "enjoy my own company" and consider myself a loner and there are many positive things that result from this, like understanding myself, really meditating on my purpose and honing how my gifts can be used to achieve it, having time to spend doing things I enjoy, and being able to really focus when I need to without distraction. On the other hand, however, I recognize the need in my life to develop emotionally secure relationships that contribute to my overall health and wellbeing.

These relationships have been essential to my growth. Why? Because the path toward inner truth, finding your purpose, and walking into your destiny, can be at times exhausting and you will need the support of others. You will need them for their emotional support, discernment, encouragement, and to remind you how strong and courageous you are. You will need them to keep you from giving up when this journey gets to be overwhelming and I can 100% guarantee you that those times will come.

What I have begun to learn with the help of intimate time with God and conversation with those in my life I trust, is that while I often felt hurt and left out and ignored during my formative years, I also probably gave off a "don't bother me" or "I am okay" or "I'm unbothered" vibe. This vibe was in

> **"** The path toward inner truth, finding your purpose, and walking into your destiny, can be at times exhausting and you will need the support of others. **"**

essence the brick wall I had erected to shelter myself from being hurt or being vulnerable. I also used members of my family, such as my Mom, who supported, lifted, and sheltered me, as a haven. Let me take a moment here to say that when God was blessing me with a Mother, he gave me one of his choicest jewels. My mom has been my biggest supporters, my best friend, my travel partner, my fiercest warrior, and my greatest advocate throughout my entire life. She has always been the one person I could depend on no matter what I needed. She truly is now and has always been the epitome of what a mom should be to me. There are no words to describe how much I appreciate, love, and adore her.

She and those other family members I was comfortable engaging, interacting, and socializing with became my safe space. I clung to what was familiar and found the support I needed from them. I can tell you it has become so important for me even in my current journey of self-discovery and self-acceptance to cling to their love, pride, and support. For every negative comment, every negative thought I had, for every negative emotion, every hurtful action or incident, they lifted me up and showed me unconditional love. As broken as I was, they were the glue that kept me together enough to keep pushing forward every day. Their belief in me kept me going even when I didn't believe in myself. They were the first and most important members of my Power Posse.

Of course, at the time I had no idea how important their role would be to my life journey or to my current path toward living my own BIG life, but God continually reminds me of their support and the impact of their examples. Two very special family members that I admire and model myself after, were my now deceased aunts, Dorothy Augustus and Margaret Mayers. They both provided for me amazing examples of women who were committed to God and were always there to support me and the rest of our family whenever needed. No matter when I interacted with them, I felt an outpouring of love and acceptance. They were the epitome of virtue, class, grace, and excellence. They were both strong women who modeled walking through your trials and triumphs humbly, depending on faith in God, and being gracious and forgiving no matter what the circumstances.

I grew up watching my Aunt Dot, who was a successful entrepreneur, give unselfishly to others, even strangers, and be a beacon of light to everyone who was fortunate enough to know her. She was extremely kind and always gave without expecting anything in return. She often helped without broadcasting her good deeds to the world and I am sure there are many people even today who do not know the extent of her support and assistance to strangers, to her community, and to those fortunate enough to have been a part of her family. She inspired me to think of others before I thought of myself and to always be willing to help those society often overlooks. In her I saw an example of living a life that honored and followed the example of Christ. She never looked down on others and found value in every person she met. She also never made apologies for who she was and she never made me feel less than because of my size. She embraced every bit of herself and lived her life bold and unapologetically.

Although I know there were times when I'm sure she had issues to navigate and challenges to face, she always exuded joy. It was in moments that she would take me shopping for clothes that I felt my most secure. Although plus-size, she was fabulous and stylish. She took great pride in her appearance and introduced me to stores that had clothes that would fit me. It is because of her I have been able all my life to dress in a way that belied the inner turmoil I was going through due to my appearance.

My aunt Margaret was one of the kindest persons I have ever had the privilege of knowing. While very quiet and soft-spoken, she exuded an undeniable strength that I admired. Whenever we spoke, no matter what her circumstances, she always had something positive to say and always had a way of turning the conversation around so that she was focused on you and not on her. She was a hard worker, a giver, and I can never once remember a time when she complained about anything. Whenever we spoke, she always told me how proud she was of me and no matter the conversation, she always inserted the advice that, "Tomorrow is not promised to anyone" and admonished me to be sure I took care of myself. She encouraged me, affirmed me, inspired me, and never once made me feel I should be ashamed because of my weight. This was made even more special by the fact that we didn't often see each other but she always reached out to me and checked on me, always calling right when I needed to hear her voice the most. I am pretty sure she also did these check-ins with other family members as well but every call I got and all the time spent in her actual presence over the years made me feel so thankful and grateful that she was a part of my life.

Another place of safety for me was losing myself in the power of books. As an avid reader, I have always enjoyed reading and during those times of isolation as a young adult, I would often read 10-20 books a week. The public library became my sanctuary and I escaped from my reality by reading about the fictitious worlds created by other authors. It was also during this time that my love for the power of the written word was birthed, and I knew even in my teen years that I wanted to one day write my own books. When reading, I was able to immerse myself fully into the characters and story lines of other people which allowed me to temporarily disengage from my own life. Reading allowed me to explore other cultures and oftentimes I was also able to find characters who were going through things that were like my own experiences. I loved to read because it was entertaining, enjoyable, and inspirational.

I can remember when I ran across what has become one of my favorite poems by, John Donne, "For Whom the Bell Tolls/No Man is an Island". The poem reads:

No man is an island,
Entire of itself,
Every man is a piece of the continent,
A part of the main.
If a clod be washed away by the sea,
Europe is the less.
As well as if a promontory were.
As well as if a manor of thy friend's
Or of thine own were:
Any man's death diminishes me,
Because I am involved in mankind,
And therefore never send to know for whom the bell tolls;
It tolls for thee.

As someone who has been very independent and very determined to be self-sufficient and truthfully, shy away from having relationships that pushed me to be vulnerable and exposed to hurt, it has been the first few lines of this poem that I have remembered as I am pushing myself to be more open, vulnerable, and more available to letting others into my life. Does that mean I am forging ahead without any limits to who and what I allow into the inner sanctum of my heart, of course not. What it does mean is that I am completely aware of what I offer to others, and I am open to freely sharing my genuine self with those who deserve it. How do you know who those "Power Posse" people are? For me, it has meant trusting God and allowing the Holy Spirit to speak to me about who I should allow to enter our space. I say our because God resides in me and there is nothing or no one I would bring into my space that would be a danger to His presence in my life.

This requires intentional insight into what makes someone an "insider" and what would require them to remain an "outsider" in the scope of your life. Insiders are those who have shown themselves to be consistent, compassionate, compromising, respectful of your boundaries, genuine, not controlling, available, willing to celebrate you and your achievements, truthful with you even when it hurts. Insiders serve as a confidant to you but also confide in you as well, make good decisions, are not gossips, strive to be their very best and push you to do the same.

Of course, that means the outside people are those who don't meet these criteria. You will still have to communicate, interact, and engage with them on an everyday basis but you are clear about the boundaries you have created and understand which persons should have "inner" access and which ones should remain "outside". This has nothing to do with how you treat them and everything to do with protecting your peace and the steps you've made in your self-growth journey. Please understand that as you make the decisions on who should be insiders and who should be outsiders, that it is not necessary to loudly explain and inform those who you have allowed to be a part of your Power Posse that they are members, because they will know. Your actions and words will affirm for them how important they are to your life.

Always be sure that you are being as great a friend as you expect others to be.

"A man that hath friends must shew himself friendly: and there is a friend that sticketh closer than a brother".

-Proverbs 18:24

Learning how to be the friend you expect others to be is so very important and it took me some time to develop those traits in myself I expected to see exhibited in others. I was so focused on how many times I had been hurt, betrayed, or tricked into believing people were truly my friends and wanted the best for me only to find out the exact opposite. As a result of that, I was burdened by the weight of my bitterness for a very long time.

Again, this in no way excuses their behaviors but God had to help me heal and reveal to me that to attract the "inside" people I needed in my life, I had to forgive the "outside" people and move beyond the pain I had allowed them to cause me. I had to realize that I had been the warden of my own heart and that because I had been so eager to please those I admired, I had allowed those "outside" people "inside". It was my own insecurity and desire to be accepted that had led to the years and years of feeling inadequate, alone, and unworthy of love and friendship. I was a master at "pretending" I was fine being all by myself. But the reality is again, "No man is an island" and it wasn't until I allowed myself to really accept and live this truth that I began to grow and become the "friendly" person who attracted "inside" people into her life.

The understanding of how to "attract" like minded friends for me began during my freshman and sophomore years at Appalachian State University. It was during my time here that I began to find the courage to open myself up to external friendships and allow myself to trust others enough to understand the value of genuine relationships. I had to go almost 5 hours away from home to learn what it meant to be accepted and celebrated and loved by people who weren't my family. Although I didn't earn my degree there and only stayed in Boone, NC for about 3 years, it was there that I found friends who loved God and who weren't afraid to live in the truth of their relationships with Him every day. Here I found friends who would become lifelong friends! Here I began to add to and enrich my "Power Posse".

Another key thing about living BIG is the understanding that you are constantly evolving and the willingness to grow and change is critical to your future success. In this same way, understand that your Power Posse will also change periodically and that is okay. Power Posse members that are here today may not be here tomorrow. Does that mean they weren't meant to be inside people? Not at all, it simply means that life shifts have meant that you and your posse member must now grow in a different direction. It means you take the positives that your posse membership has brought about, and you use it to enhance and support others you meet and who become a part of your posse and prayerfully, those past members will do the same. Never be afraid to allow a Power Posse member to flourish and spread their own wings. Send them off with love and support them as they have supported you because the reality is, your success and your destiny is linked to theirs.

Relationships, no matter, who they are with, change and develop over time just like you do as a person. They require effort on our part to grow and maintain them. With those God-ordained relationships you value, always remain open by sharing your thoughts, and feelings. Relationships cannot survive when they are one-sided, they must be an equal balance between give and take by both parties involved in them. A few years ago, I had a relationship with a very special friend to me end abruptly. In processing the pain of that, I began to realize that although I had often given of myself and been there to support the person no matter when they needed me, this behavior had not been reciprocated. At special times in my life, at the painful times when I needed their presence, they simply were not there.

So as difficult as it was to do, when that person disappeared from my life, I made the decision to allow them to be gone. There will be many times in this journey to being your best you that you will also have to do the same. Relationships thrive on and require connection and this connection can only be established by always being willing to share your true and authentic self with those around you but being confident that they are also doing the same. If not, be courageous enough to challenge them on their own journeys to be authentic and provide a space where they feel free to also be themselves around you.

One of the hardest aspects of relationship building that I have had to work on is being available. As a result of my earlier coping mechanism of keeping to myself and being a loner, it is second nature for me to just stay to myself. But remember what I said earlier, relationships can't be one sided. When you give your time to others you are essentially solidifying their value to your life.

Simply put, when the people around you feel as if you WANT to spend time with them, they know that you value and appreciate your presence in their life. They know that you truly do care about them.

> **"**
> Relationships cannot survive when they are one-sided, they must be an equal balance between give and take by both parties involved in them.
> **"**

This means showing up for each other and not expecting the other person to do all the work to keep the relationship going. Because I had been so wounded in my younger relationships by those I felt I could trust, this was really hard for me to do. Being available meant I also had to be vulnerable, and I did not want to expose myself to potentially being hurt by other people ever again. It was only through my relationship with God that I have been able to open myself up even more because I know that He covers, protects, and keeps me and that no matter what, He will be there for me to guide me and comfort me if needed.

Another key behavior which is needed in relationships is respect. I cannot tell you the number of times I have experienced someone who is disrespectful to others demand they be given respect. I am sure I have probably even been guilty of this in my own life, and I am sure you have too, but if we are going to develop healthy mutually beneficial relationships, respect is something that must be both given and received. You must respect the opinion, feelings, time, and life journey of others around you. It will be important and helpful to establish boundaries because they will be critical to developing a healthy habit of respectful engagement.

Listen to your Power Posse members about what they need and honestly verbalize what you need from them. You should know and understand what things are okay and what things are absolute deal breakers when it comes to establishing healthy relationships with them. Be willing to share your dreams, visions, values, and   beliefs with them. Power Posse members will always create an environment where you are safe to do so without passing judgement and without demeaning you.

Lastly, please understand that there will never be a relationship where you agree with everything a person does, thinks, or feels. There will be times when you disagree even with those you consider "insiders". You are a genuine and unique being, remember we discussed this in previous chapters. God only made one of you in the entire world, therefore you will think and act differently from everyone around you. You will have your own beliefs, thoughts, emotions, dreams, and desires. You need Power Posse members who are confident enough to disagree with you in times when those thoughts, emotions, dreams, and desires impede your growth, lead you down a destructive path, or hinder your purpose pursuit. In the same way, you should be able to freely do the same for them.

Unhealthy   relationships   thrive   when   there   is   poor communication. Be willing to freely embrace your differences and the times when those differences lead to healthy conflict. Healthy conflict involves providing and receiving feedback that is rooted in a desire to uplift and not tear down those around you. It will result in stimulating and thought-provoking conversations that result in shifting you to a higher level of personal growth. Let's be honest here, we as people, are sometimes just messy. As a result, there will be times when you or a member of your Power Posse will say or do something that hurts or angers you or you will do something that hurts or angers them.

In those times, it is important to navigate the relationship by remembering why you have trusted that person to be an "insider" in your life. Be vulnerable enough to deal with the conflict head on and maturely get to the root of the issue to find a resolution that builds each person up and allows for compromise.

> **"** Healthy conflict involves providing and receiving feedback that is rooted in a desire to uplift and not tear down those around you. **"**

My prayer for you as you begin to build your "Power Posse" is that you cultivate relationships that honor God, that are loving, healthy, and long-lasting. Remember that you are not a perfect being and our relationships will at times reflect our imperfections. Doing the work however to authentically live your BIG life will mean an increased ability for you to be a better person both for yourself and for those you love.

Prayer #7: Dear Heavenly Father, I thank you so much for always being there for me and for showing me what true love is. I am so grateful for your presence, and I humbly come before you to ask that you would create in me a heart and mind to develop and cultivate God-ordained relationships which bring you honor. Please take away all the pain and hurt from previous broken relationships and allow my relationships to be filled with patience, mutual respect, love, and understanding. Please bring people into my life that will be a source of companionship and friendship that encourage me as I provide the same for them. Help me to be the friend you have called me to be, one who exhibits your character in all I do and speak. Teach me to cultivate quality relationships and to always show up in my authentic self genuinely. Help me to release relationships which are detrimental to my health and well-being. Please guide me, purify my heart, and build my character. I thank you Lord for your guidance and your faithfulness and love. I fully submit to you and thank you for leading me and showing me what true love is. In Jesus' name I pray, Amen.

BIG Step #7: Create a list of 5-10 characteristics you would like members of your Power Posse to possess. Next, beside each trait, write 1-2 sentences describing the ways in which you exhibit that trait in your own personal life. Spend some time reflecting on and praying over your list and begin to identify those around you who you consider your "insiders". It is okay if all those people don't currently exist, remember we are believing for God-ordained relationships in your life. Think of a way that you can share with each of the people you've identified how much their relationship means to you and ask for their support as you continue your journey to Living BIG. Be specific with ways in which they can help you be accountable to your goals and walking in your purpose. Think of how you can intentionally "show up" in some small way this week for them. Will it be a kind unexpected gesture? A phone call? An invite to lunch? No matter what you decide, be sure you follow through and then journal how you felt afterwards.

Journal Entry #7: Consider the relationships in your life currently. For those that are positive and healthy, in what ways have you felt supported and how have you supported them? How do you spend time with them and how often? How can you be more intentional with your time? In what ways are you alike and in what ways are you different? How can you become a better spouse, parent, child, sibling, or friend?

Conclusion

*Live Your **BIG** (Bold, Inspired, & Gifted) Life Now!*

I pray that as you have read the chapters, prayed the prayers, completed the BIG Step activities, and journaled your thoughts in this book that you feel empowered to do the following things:

- Look in the mirror and be honest about who you are holistically and embrace your WHOLE authentic self, the things you appreciate and the things you don't, the things you want to keep and the things you want to change.

- Realize that seeing them, understanding them, working on them, and embracing them all allow you to become the BIG person God designed you to be.

- Quiet the negative voices you've allowed to dictate your view of yourself in the past. Tune into the person God says you are by spending time in His word and in prayer.

- Be willing to confess and acknowledge your faults and allow God to help you correct them. Consistently check in with Him to be sure your attitudes and actions don't sabotage your progress or your journey.

I pray that the seven essential steps I have shared will aid you in starting, walking through, and welcoming your journey toward living bold, inspired, and gifted (BIG):

1. Facing YOUR Truth: The Looking Glass
2. Being the best YOU, you can be, not the YOU others expect you to be.
3. Embracing the positives and change the negatives.
4. Releasing the Past, Walking into YOUR future!
5. Celebrating YOU! Small Steps Really Matter.
6. Pursuing YOUR passion, Finding YOUR purpose.
7. Saddle Up YOUR Power Posse.

There is a unique path that you are being called to walk, unique gifts that you are meant to share with the world, a unique personality and outlook that will help someone heal, a unique story that will help others as they overcome their own personal life obstacles, and your unique voice that will uplift, empower, and inspire the world. Be courageous enough to show up for yourself because every day that you spend overlooking, not accepting, and not understanding the beautiful gifts that God has given you means more days that you choose to live small and not bold, inspired, and gifted (BIG). More importantly, it means the people you have been called by God to help reach their own destinies are at risk to fail. Yes, your purpose is just that important! YOU are just that important! You are the key to someone else's greatness and whether they succeed or fail rests in your commitment to taking the journey to heal past your hurt and FINALLY starting the journey to walking fully in your purpose.

Thank You

Thank you for reading Living BIG: Bold, Inspired & Gifted (Shattering the Looking Glass to Embrace the Greatness Within). I truly hope you enjoyed it and that the principles shared within will provide you with the courage you need to embrace your BIG life and share your authentic amazing self with the world!

Please do take the time to:
Write a verified Amazon review!
Your written opinion is important because your voice matters, and I welcome the opportunity for you to inspire others to read the book and transform their lives by Living BIG!

Visit my website www.vernamayersfakunle.com and subscribe to receive news, updates, and special offers.